UNIQUELY AMERICAN

LESLIE ELENA WOLF

ARPress

ARPress
45 Dan Road Suite 5
Canton MA 02021
Hotline: 1(888) 821-0229
Fax: 1(508) 545-7580

Ordering Information:
Quantity sales. Special discounts are available on quantity purchases by corporations, associations, and others. For details, contact the publisher at the address above.

Printed in the United States of America.

ISBN-13:   Softcover   979-8-89676-542-4
                 eBook   979-8-89676-543-1

Library of Congress Control Number: 2024927257

TABLE OF CONTENTS

Dedicated to women and men
in the United States National Guard—
I love you.

PREFACE

After serving over 30 years in the Idaho National Guard, I have become accustomed to the civilian population not understanding the National Guard. I have deployed twice to Iraq, spent two and a half years in Cambodia as part of the State Partnership Program, and served in various positions. My experience taught me that the National Guard's budgets and laws pertaining to its various statuses were complicated.

However, it was not until I returned home from Senior Service College in Newport, Rhode Island, in 2021 that I accidentally found the 2001 book *I Am the Guard* by Michael D. Doubler on the National Guard director's website. I realized I knew little about the Guard outside my own experiences. The American people had just funded my full-time education in Newport, and I'd loved every bit of it (except having Zoom classes because of COVID-19). Still, I had spent a year studying military history and strategy but knew little about my organization.

At this point, I was curious about the evolution of the Guard and frustrated with the lack of Guard-focused professional development. I dove into Mr. Doubler's book with a mission: to learn more about the Guard that I loved.

I saw a pattern of tension in the book: the tension between the state and federal government and the tension and competition between the Regular Army and the National Guard. As I kept reading, I grew prouder of my organization and more curious. However, the book was written before the War on Terror, so it lacked two decades of the Guard's history in combat in the Middle East.

I began researching a history I had only heard select stories about, such as the highly controversial Kent State incident and other landmark examples of civil unrest that put the National Guard in the middle. Some of the stories were shameful, such as a Native American massacre in Colorado in 1864, during which the militia mutilated and scalped nearly 150 tribespeople while their warriors were away. I was absorbed by the National Guard's involvement in the War on Drugs and the Waco Siege in 1993. Other stories, such as that of the 2nd Battalion, 138th Field Artillery unit from the Kentucky National Guard, put tears in my eyes. The 2nd Battalion, 138th was one of the few units to deploy during the Vietnam War. The unit was so effective that the Viet Cong sappers attacked their firebase to destroy them. Despite their sneak attack, the enemy could not succeed in their mission. However, in that battle, the citizens in the small town of Bardstown, Kentucky, suffered heavy losses.

That's how it is in the Guard, then and now. Just like in the Revolutionary War, the Guardsmen in 2023 supporting Operation Spartan Shield deploy alongside their neighbors, friends, and relatives. As it was with the early militia, the bond between service members in the National Guard is very strong.

I also found the history behind the Guard prejudice was deep and went back to the days of Federalists and Anti-Federalists. Individuals such as Major General Upton created an anti-Guard culture at West Point and in the professional Army. However, the Guard had its champions, such as John Palmer and the National Guard Association, acting as strong proponents for Guard policy improvements. The competition between the Active Duty and Guard continues even in 2023, as the budget gets tight and the Guard competes for a Space National Guard.

What I found most interesting was the ongoing relevance of the National Guard in politics today, as we continue to face the same debates. For example, the political tensions between the state government and the federal government, putting the National Guard in the middle, goes back to the War of 1812 and has never really ceased. The headlines of 2023 seem to revisit the same debate. In 2021, Governor DeSantis of Florida created a State Guard that is completely funded with state resources and only under his control—the State Defense Force.

Some might think the State Defense Force is politically controversial. However, there are actually 18 other states with State Defense Forces to support their governors with domestic operations. The State Defense Force does not answer to the Pentagon or the National Guard Bureau, and the governor does not have to share his forces for combat operations overseas.

Through this State Guard, Governor DeSantis planned to supplement the Florida National Guard, which has federal and state missions.[1] I found these political tensions captivating.

In fact, the more I learned about the Guard's long history, the more fascinated I was. These stories have to be told before it is too late and the American people become completely disconnected from the National Guard and military.

The Departure of the Guard from the People

In Gary Hart's book, *The Minuteman: Returning to an Army of the People,* he states that the military has become separate and distant from the American people. This phenomenon, he claims, began during the Cold War. He writes, "… isolation of the military from society is unhealthy at best and dangerous at worst."[2] He states that the best way to engage the American people in military policy that affects their lives is to place greater reliance on the citizen-soldier.[3]

The National Guard is the military connection to civilian employers, community members, and local businesses, and provides all Americans an opportunity to sacrifice and contribute to America's Wars.

Hart writes, "Virtually all theoreticians of republican government have discussed the dangers of maintaining a permanent standing army in time of peace and the importance of a national militia."[4]

In the past, the National Guard kept the dialog about our national security at the local, state, and federal levels. With families, employers, Guard, and Reservists impacted by conflicts in remote corners of the

---

1

2 *Hart, Gary. The Minuteman: Returning to an Army of the People.* Free Press, 2011, p. 12.

3 Ibid., pg. 15

4 Ibid., pg. 21

world, elected officials were more likely to be called upon to explain the US military's involvement and how it related to our national security objectives.[5]

Foreign and military policies are not so complicated that they must be left to the elites; the discussion belongs in the realm of the American people. The Guard used to keep the American people engaged. I believe that changed during the Vietnam War.

In August 2023, a Gallup poll found that American confidence in the military had reached its lowest point in 25 years.[6] This is a shame, but I can understand. In the last couple of years, I have faced the reality that the 20 years of the War on Terror in Iraq were based on falsehoods and political propaganda. I was shocked when I saw the August 2021 withdrawal from Afghanistan. It was a travesty and left me feeling sick to my stomach.

However, I wish the American people could see what I see in the National Guard: the citizen-soldiers that volunteer to protect their communities domestically and overseas. They come from all demographics and vast backgrounds. They are following orders handed down to them from the Pentagon's professional officers and political leaders. Our citizen-soldiers deserve the best military and civilian leadership. I wish the American people would be more engaged in the activities of the National Guard and demand the best leadership at the national level.

The Guard's desired position in our country and communities is fading away. The Guard is the connection between civilians and our democratic form of government because we all know—or *are*—a relative, friend, co-worker, or neighbor who serves. The National Guard is a uniquely American military we should all be proud of.

I hope this book sheds light on and stirs curiosity about America's Guard and the citizen-soldiers.

---

5   Ibid., pg. 16

6   Drew, Lawrence F. "Public's Confidence in the Military Drops Again." *Military News*, 1 Aug. 2023, military.com/daily-news/2023/08/01/confidence-military-reaches-new-25-year-low.html.

CHAPTER 1

————— ❧ —————

Introduction to the National Guard Dilemma

"Always Ready, Always There!"

—National Guard slogan

The National Guard is a uniquely American military force. No other army like it exists in the world.

The roots of the National Guard are in the militia, a self-defense and preservation system the colonial pilgrims brought over from Europe. The citizen-soldier concept is ancient and can be traced back to ancient Greece and Rome. The evolution of the historical American colonial militia into the modern-day National Guard, with its dual mission, is the product of our constitutional republic and the inherent tensions built into the system.

The story of the American citizen-soldier is a story of passion: sacrificing one's own time, resources, and even one's life to go into combat to protect one's family, community, freedom, and way of life. History has shown that citizen-soldiers with good leadership can defeat the best professional army.

Throughout the United States' history of militia and, later, the National Guard, we find stories in which the soldiers may have lacked discipline, training, or equipment, resulting in unexpected damages or even injuries or deaths. Further investigation reveals the underlying implications of such incidents and the complex challenges these soldiers overcame as a part-time force.

The citizen-soldier in the National Guard has been in the middle of political stand-offs between governors and presidents. The National Guard leaders fought for existence against those advocating for only federal armed forces. In addition, the Constitution, state and federal laws, and tradition itself have limited the use of the militia and National Guard.

The National Guard of today is the result of decades of men and women on the ground overcoming limited training, logistics capabilities, equipment, and funding to achieve mission success. The Guard of today was not the vision of the Founding Fathers, but neither were the Regular Army or professional soldiers.

The National Guard is the story of American rise to hegemony. As the United States' worldwide power and influence increased, so did the need for a powerful military. However, America's foundation grew organically from recognizing the danger of a large and powerful standing army in the hands of despotic leadership. The debate over the size and funding of a standing army versus a citizen-soldiers force is endless.

The National Guard secured its place as a reserve for the standing Army through America's wars and ongoing support. In other words, the Regular Army can't go to war very long without using the National Guard. They need the Guard's capacity or the capability. So, the National Guard must train to the same standards as the Regular forces and have the same military equipment to integrate seamlessly. This means that the National Guard is primarily sustained with federal funding.

To standardize all the independent state militias, the states needed money, and a lot of it. Congress realized the necessity of sending funds to the states but required the Regular Army to oversee the militia and, later, the National Guard.

The National Guard is a part-time force that consists mainly of citizen-soldiers. There's a member of the National Guard in nearly every ZIP code. They are locals from every community, friends and neighbors, employers and employees, parents and children, teachers and students. They can be called to action whenever needed and will respond with valor. We see and know these men and women in the community in grocery stores, gas stations, schools, social events, charities, and town events. National Guard soldiers have deep roots and vested interests in their communities.

The National Guard Today[7]

The citizen-soldier provides a vital link to America's global conflicts and is designed to keep the American people vested in foreign policy, giving the American people more insight and the ability to hold elected officials accountable. There is an apparent reason: when a citizen-soldier deploys, more community members must sacrifice and take notice: an important person has gone to serve, and we notice both their absence and recognize their sacrifice and ours. In theory, the more people must make sacrifices, the more engaged the community will be in foreign policy and our elected leadership's decisions.

What do you imagine when you think of domestic matters to which the National Guard responds? Disaster relief? Policing at public gatherings? That's correct—but there is so much more. You may be unaware of how much work the National Guard does nationwide. Over the last five chaotic years alone, they've served a record ten million days in domestic missions, aiding the COVID-19 pandemic, controlling wildfires that have been increasingly ravaging North America, supporting communities before and after natural weather disasters such as hurricanes, and serving at the front lines of civil disturbances.

The Guard's COVID-19 response was heroic. They distributed hundreds of millions of meals and the same amount of protective gear to essential workers. At the height of the pandemic, the Guard tested over sixteen million people for the virus nationwide, administering well over 100,000 vaccinations a day.

The National Guard also:

- Helps keep our airspace safe.

- Maintains stable communications between our local, state, and federal emergency agencies.

---

7   Data in this section is from *Year of the Guard; 2022 National Guard Bureau Posture Statement: A Record Year of Being Always Ready, Always There.*

- Forms multiple battalions of people devoted to CBRN response (Chemical, Biological, Radiological, and Nuclear).

But even if you don't see the National Guard on the streets, they always protect America behind the scenes. Recently, they've taken over $10 billion of illicit drugs and weaponry off the streets. They train Department of Defense (DOD) personnel.

They even form a considerable chunk of our nation's cybersecurity efforts, creating 59 cyber units in over 40 states. For example, over a thousand members detected 57 "vulnerability events" during the 2020 election. They support IT infrastructure, vulnerability assessments, network monitoring, and traffic.

For cases of severe weather, including earthquakes, flooding, tornadoes, hurricanes, and winter storms, the National Guard distributes food to those separated from their homes or rendered homeless. The Guard clears the damaged and impassable roads through disaster areas so that more relief can arrive. They distribute water and set up makeshift shelters for those in need.

The National Guard also has a significant role in our military; they back up and support the regular US Federal forces worldwide. The Guard comprises 39% of the United States' operational forces. This support includes:

- 300,000 soldiers

- 8 divisions

- 27 combat teams

- 42 multifunctional brigades

- 56 functional support brigades and groups

- 13 command and control headquarters

- Over 1,000 aircraft

- Tens of thousands of infrastructural buildings, including over 100 training centers in thousands of communities.

Note that these numbers cover only the Army's support. There is an equivalent National Guard reinforcement presence in the Air Force, and they even provide operational capability to the Space Force. The National Guard includes both the Air National Guard and Army National Guard; this book will focus on the evolution and tensions in the Army National Guard.

Summary of Contents

We will explore the following topics:

Chapter Two begins with a story of early citizen-soldiers called hoplites and the Battle of Marathon. The famous battle was pivotal for not only ancient Greece but also modern democracy and Western culture. The early heroes that paved the way for the culture and lifestyle we enjoy today were the Athenian citizens and their ingenuity over the professional warriors of Persia.

The chapter then turns to the history of the militia and the need for citizens to protect themselves and their property from danger. Colonial Americans brought the militia tradition from Europe. They knew the community where they lived was the first line—often the only line—of defense.

We will observe the connection between the Constitution and the militia, the limits the Constitution had on the militia in foreign wars, and the laws that tried to correct that. We'll chart the history of the militia from the Revolutionary War to the National Defense Act of 1916, which officially named the National Guard.

Chapter Three continues the discussion on the evolution of the National Guard into the 20th century. The Guard was in high demand and proudly served in World War I, II, and the Korean War. Important legislation passed in 1956 created the Title 10 and Title 32 US Codes for the Regular military and National Guard. The chapter dives into the Vietnam War and President Johnson's decision to leave most of the National Guard behind. This decision ignored the combat success of the Guard in the past. In 1991, the Bush administration opted to leave the Guard combat units out of the ground offensive in Kuwait.

By this time, the friction between the federal levels of government and between the Regular Army and National Guard was well established.

Chapter Four examines the state and federal tensions with the National Guard in the middle. This chapter concerns the political tension between the state governors and the United States President. For example, several governors refused to send their militias to fight in the War of 1812, the Civil War, the 1950s desegregation battles, or South America in the 1980s. These are all examples of historical tensions between the governor and president that put the Guard in the middle, and we have yet to see a resolution to these complex rivalries. More recent examples include the battle over the southern border and COVID-19 policies.

Chapter Five concerns the tensions between the professional Army (the United States' full-time force) and the weekend warriors or the National Guard. The tensions began at the political level at our country's founding between the Federalists and the Anti-Federalists. The Federalists wanted a full-time professional force, while their opponents were firmly against the idea. The chapter goes through the Guard's champions and rivals and the disagreements between the components during World War I, II, and the Cold War. This brings us to modern times when we finally see the National Guard sitting on the Joint Chiefs of Staff.

Chapter Six regards the National Guard and civil unrest in the United States. The history of civil unrest goes back to Samuel Adams and the patriots who pushed against British rule. The chapter spans from Shay's Rebellion to the labor disputes in 1877.

Chapter Seven brings us into the modern era of civil unrest, from the turbulent social change riots of the 1960s to the disaster at Kent State in 1970 to the 2020 riots following the death of George Floyd. The chapter concludes by noting the National Guard's support to other government agencies, including the War on Drugs and the tragedy at Waco, Texas, in 1993.

Chapter Eight is the conclusion, in which we will examine where the National Guard came from.

Summary

This book will explore our unique American National Guard, a military force with one boot in combat and the other in domestic operations, born out of necessity. Yet its existence came with inherent tensions created through the Constitution.

My overall purpose is not to disparage the Regular Army or those who serve; we need a standing Army. Nor do I wish to criticize the American federal system. Instead, my aim is to underscore the connection of the citizen-soldier to a representative republic.

The National Guard is governed by a set of laws that are complex and largely misunderstood by the American people. This book aims to highlight the evolution and fascinating history of the National Guard and demonstrate that the Guard's ongoing complexities mirror the country it sprang from. The heart and spirit of America is represented in the National Guard.

CHAPTER 2

❧

Early Evolution of the National Guard

Marathon

The Battle of Marathon (490 BC) is a cornerstone event in Western civilization.

Like all empires, the vast Persian Empire expanded (and ruled for over two centuries) because of conquest, and Persian forces were infamously unbeatable. At the time of the battle, the Persian Empire's control extended across ancient Europe, including Thrace and Macedonia, and Greece was their next target. Their emperor, Darius, had already pushed his forces onto Greek shores and was heading with purpose toward the city-state of Athens.

The Athenian army rushed to meet them on the fields around the town of Marathon to block Persian passage inland. Athens appealed to the mighty Greek city-state of Sparta for reinforcements, but Sparta was delayed in sending troops because of a religious festival. Sparta was the most capable Greek city-state for taking on Persia, as it had a large professional warrior class. However, waiting for Sparta was not an option for Athens. They would have to hold the Persians at bay in Marathon for ten days on their own.

The Athenians were the underdogs facing a significantly more powerful force. To meet this challenge, the Athenians had to call on all available hoplites.

The backbone of the Athenian military was the hoplite soldier. The hoplites were citizen-soldiers armed with spears and shields and trained to battle in phalanx formation. Their combination of shields and spear-positions enabled them to provide more defensive protection with fewer soldiers. The hoplites were not professionals; but were largely property owners and free, skilled artisans.

Just like in colonial America, the people of Athens were everyday men and women fighting for themselves, arming themselves "against a sea of troubles," as Shakespeare might put it. Being a citizen-soldier was a duty expected from those who enjoyed the privilege of their nation's care.

The hoplites, being invested citizens of the culture, understood that their way of life and freedom was on the line. On the day of the battle, the hoplites were greatly outnumbered, though the exact numbers of the Persian army are historically uncertain. At the most generous estimate, the Greeks were outnumbered at least two to one, and chances of victory seemed slim. The hoplites were admired for their skills as soldiers, but they rarely fought; they were essentially part-time, only mustered as needed. They were men fighting not for money but for their homeland, their honor, and the future of their city-state's culture.

Like the militia and the National Guard, the hoplites often fought side-by-side with their families or neighbors. These men weren't just fighting for their kings and rulers but for their future and for the ones they loved. A hoplite used his shield not to protect himself but to protect the man next to him. Their formations required a great deal of trust and discipline.

With superior tactics and steadfast morale, the Greeks managed to defeat the Persians in a bloody battle. Though this is an admittedly simplified retelling of the battle, essentially, Persian archers and troops were unable to penetrate the hoplites' hard phalanx formations or respond to the hand-to-hand combat in which the hoplites were trained. The Greek army set up an almost entirely defensive position, meaning the Persian attackers had to come to them. This battle was won by part-time warriors, accomplishing the impossible with cleverness fueled by their passion.

This victory marked the rise of the Athenian city-state, but the victory also shifted beliefs when it came to conquering the Persians. It was now proven that the Persians could indeed be driven back. Victory over the Persians ensured democracy, free markets, and Western culture would spread; thus, the battle was pivotal to the freedoms and liberties enjoyed around the world today.

This battle was vital in expanding Western thought. Later, the colonial militia fighting in the French and Indian War would follow the Greeks' example by building confidence in their citizen-soldiers' military capabilities.

The Athenian hoplites paved the way for democracy, liberty, and unimaginable innovation; the colonial militia did the same in the 18th century. The liberties and freedoms we enjoy in the Western world only exist because of our citizen-soldiers and their traditions.

Fight For Your Life

To grasp the special quality of the National Guard as an institution, it is crucial to understand how the organization began and then adapted. The world, and the concept and requirements of service, changed around it, contributing to the National Guard as we know it today.

We begin our story by considering the evolution of the citizen-soldier.

People have always needed protection, from wildlife, natural disasters, or enemies seeking to take their lives or land. For the larger part of human history, there was one sort of protection available: we picked up a weapon and protected what was ours. If we could not do so, our land and life were likely forfeited to something bigger, stronger, or more determined than us.

When enemies were at the gate, able-bodied people responded because that was the only option.

Small groups of humans living together and forming communities had the benefit of sufficient population to begin dividing duties among the citizens. If there weren't enough people to commission an army, they nevertheless saw the benefit of assigning "citizen-soldier" duties to certain people so that others could continue agriculture or other work necessary to keep the community functioning. Thus, some people prepared to be "at the ready."

Such groups were called militia, a term that encompasses a group of citizens with some limited military training who could be called upon to respond to emergencies. The idea of a militia is worldwide, and many cultures can find militia groups playing significant roles in historical conflicts. There are plenty of good stories in which a dedicated, dug-in, and stubbornly patriotic militia fended off what seemed like far greater foes. In the United States, we are most familiar with our own Revolutionary War, in which our militia faced off against the most well-trained, well-equipped army in the world—the British redcoats.

The Guard and the US Constitution

People might take the dual nature of the National Guard for granted, in its service of the federal and state governments, perhaps assuming it's always been this way. In fact, the National Guard's service to the governor and the president was an evolution away from the original intent of the Constitution.

The Massachusetts colonial legislature established the militia/National Guard about 140 years before Congress established the Regular Army. The early Americans believed a citizen-soldier force was not only needed for defense but also essential for a free people, just like the men who came forward to serve Athens.

Our Founding Fathers created a democratic republic with a defense system based on the obligation of its citizens to protect their community, just like the Grecian hoplites. The Constitution created a federal system with state militias and allowed Congress to raise an Army and Navy, as needed, for no more than two years. However, while the Constitution created the militia, it also created obstacles to using the militia/National Guard as a global force.

As the United States increased its global dominance, the demand for a regular Army also increased. For the National Guard to support national security interests overseas, it had to overcome various limitations imposed by the Constitution. Congress, supported by an active lobbying effort, had to pass new laws.

A discussion about the evolution of the National Guard must start with the Constitution adopted in 1787. I hope to show that the evolution of the Guard is uniquely American. A remarkable citizen-soldier force emerged through a hodgepodge of laws to make the National Guard a strategic reserve, then later an operational reserve, for the Regular Army.

A strategic reserve is a force that used to augment the Regular Army during a major combat operation. In the past, this was normally once in a generation, like World War I, II, and Korea.

During the War on Terror, the Guard changed to an operational reserve. This means that the Guard is a force actively participating in ongoing operations around the globe alongside the Regular Army. As you can see, a significant shift in the demand put on the citizen-solder training part-time.

Understanding this history is essential to comprehend the various uses of the National Guard domestically and overseas.

It is also essential to understand that the militia/National Guard is a military of the people. It's a vital link to our communities and our government representatives.

Anne Armstrong, JD, argues the National Guard is the best military model for a democratic republic, not because of the affordability but because of the moral and ethical responsibility of citizenship: *"Kant's theory of higher moral duty - one that results in a universal law of fairness and non-manipulation of one's fellow man to an end-does, in fact, readily apply to the Citizen-Soldier concept in a democratic republic such as the United States."*[8]

The modern Guard can be viewed through the lens of the enlightenment and rule by the people. This is clearly seen in the Constitution preamble, which states, *"We the People of the United States, In Order to form a more*

---

8   Armstrong, Anne. "We hold these truths to be self-evident: The National Guard and the Categorial Imperative." *Digital Georgetown*, 2019, https://repository.library.georgetown.edu/handle/10822/1056008.

perfect Union, establish Justice, ensure domestic Tranquility, <u>provide for the common defense</u>, promote the general Welfare, and secure the Blessings of Liberty to ourselves and our Posterity, do ordain and establish this Constitution for the United States of America."

The Articles of Confederation were replaced by the US Constitution because, within those Articles, political power was weighed heavily on states, resulting in a very weak central government. However, the fear of a powerful central government was still in the minds of the Anti-Federalists. As a result of the debates and compromises between the Federalists and the Anti-Federalists, the Constitution was created. While the Constitution was genius, it started a nation of mini-militias that were not only hobbled in their use against foreign powers but lacked conformity.

The following Articles, Sections, and Amendments of the Constitution are important for the militia and the evolution of the modern-day National Guard:

Article I, Section 8

The Raise/Support Armies Clause states: Congress shall have the power to raise and support Armies, but no appropriation of money to that use shall be for longer term than two years.

The Militia Clause states: Congress has the power to provide for organizing, arming, and disciplining, the Militia, and for governing it in the Service of the United States, reserving to the States respectively, the appointments of the officers, and the authority of training the militia according to the discipline prescribed by Congress.

Article II, Section 2

The President shall be the Commander in Chief of the Army and Navy of the

United States, and the Militia of the several States, when called into the actual Service of the United States.

*****

The "Calling Forth Act" Amendment in 1795 gave the president the authority to call the militia into federal service, but only after he received a court order or request of assistance from a local magistrate, the state legislature, or the governor.

*****

The following language from the Amendments to the Constitution indicates that the states wanted to restrict the authority of the central government.

The Amendments start: "The Convention of a number of the States, having at the time of their adopting the Constitution, expressed a desire, in order to prevent misconstruction or abuse of its powers, that further declaratory and restrictive clauses should be added: And as extending the ground of public confidence in the Government, will best ensure the beneficent ends of its institution."

Amendment II

A well-regulated Militia, being necessary to the security of a free State, the right of the people to keep and bear Arms, shall not be infringed.

Amendment IX

The powers not delegated to the
United States by the Constitution,
nor prohibited by it to the States, are
reserved to the States respectively, or to
the people.

The American Revolutionary War

The American Revolutionary War was the birth of a new kind of
soldier. A colonial man might be plowing his field one day, and the
next day must act as a soldier, one of conviction, principle, loyalty to
his country, and duty to his family. For him, failure was not an option.

After the British Civil War in 1651, the early American colonists
preferred dispersed citizen-soldiers to a standing army. The distrust
of the central authority and standing army ran deep in the DNA of
the first colonists—for why else would they have elected to leave their
homeland to form a new way of life?

The colonists relied on the militia tradition from Britain. Men between
certain age groups were obligated to serve their community militia part-
time. The requirement to serve became known as the "enrolled militia."
Just like the British compulsory service, the colonial requirement was
normally limited in time and within a specific area.

Colonial legislatures required towns or villages to meet a quota of male
"volunteers." This provided bodies with which the federal government
could augment the standing provincial army. Such men were used for
regional emergencies such as the French and Indian War (1754-1763).

Even at this early stage, there were questions of fairness in the system.
For example, men who didn't want to join the provincials could pay
a fine, asking the town to hire a substitute to fill their requirements.
Therefore, many provincial forces were made up of the poor; wealthy and
influential citizens tended to slough off their provincial requirements
to men who needed the money. The gap between the citizens who
served and those who didn't established a foothold.

The provincials were used in combination with, and supplementally to, British soldiers. While they had some successes, the British saw the provincial military as undisciplined and ragtag. Remember, these provincial forces were among the lower economic class; they were not the colonial militia. The British mistakenly believed the provincial military was the same as the colonial militia. They didn't understand the cohesiveness and passion behind their militia fighting.

Militia Act of 1792

The United States Congress passed the Militia Act of 1792, which required every able-bodied man between 18 and 45 to serve in an enrolled militia. These men had to provide their own weapons and equipment, as the law provided no federal money.

The Militia Act created guidance on standards and norms for states regarding their militias. Federal service was not to exceed three months, and the men serving were to be used only domestically to enforce laws, repel invasion, and suppress insurrections. Future conflicts would reveal that the Act lacked compliance mechanisms and did not define the militia as a reserve force for the Regular Army. More importantly, it blocked the use of the militia in foreign wars.

The enlightenment ideals of citizenship duty are clear in the early defense. However, state legislatures could authorize deferments based on men's occupations. As time passed, it became easier for affluent men to avoid service. While some deferments were necessary, the situation planted the seeds of having a professional warrior class and a class of citizens with no skin in the fight.

After the second war with Britain in 1812, the focus on the enrolled militia declined. The population of men in our new country grew. It became impossible to resource and train *all* men between 18 and 45. Because the wealthy could pay a fine and avoid musters, resentment over the process spread.

If a war did break out, the men available far exceeded the need. The universal service obligation created a situation that depleted readiness. So, by 1840, the enrolled militia became obsolete. Yet war, and the need to augment the Regular Army, did not.

The Civil War and Beyond

During the United States Civil War, President Lincoln tried to use the quota system to fill the needs of the Union Army. The system was inadequate because of the high casualty rates from combat and disease. Both the Union and Confederacy initiated a draft, but the quota system was still in existence. A state quota system was based on governors providing a certain number of men to fight (regardless of their military skills), not on unit capability. The process relied on the governors complying with the executive branch. The ability of the governors to block the use of their militias and, later, the National Guard over political differences resulted in more reliance on a professional Army controlled at the federal level.

Further tensions arose when, once again, those with wealth or influence could avoid service. The Civil War was sometimes called "a rich man's war and a poor man's fight."[9] All men ages 20-45 were required to enroll, and districts had quotas to keep, which would be filled via lotteries if the enrollment didn't meet the quota. When names were selected by lottery, these men had three choices:

1. Fight

2. Find someone to take their spot (for pay or some other benefit)

3. Pay a $300 commutation fee, which eliminated them from the draft

Some doctors could be bribed to declare a man unfit for fighting; some men simply ran away to avoid fighting. Overall, it seemed that the wealthy had the advantage: they could pay to excuse themselves from the bloody side of the war. This resulted in dramatically increased tensions and a sad diminishing of patriotism. How could belief in the patriotic duty to fight for one's country survive with the burden of sacrifice being shifted to the poor?

The Spanish-American War was triggered after the Spanish sunk the USS Maine in the Havana harbor in 1898. President McKinley returned to the familiar practice of putting quotas on states. He required the first

---

9   Golding, C. "Civil War 150: A rich man's war and a poor man's fight." *Ford's Theatre*, 2013, https://fords.org/civil-war-150-a-rich-mans-war-and-a-poor-mans-fight/.

quota to come from the militia. Because of the potential restriction on using the militia overseas, the militiamen had to "volunteer" for foreign duty.

The militia volunteers lacked adequate training and equipment because of the lack of standards and funding in the states. Many men were still deployed with obsolete rifles, while the regular forces were equipped with more modern magazine-fed rifles.

Regardless, the American people were proud of their citizen-soldiers' performance in the Spanish-American War. Americans in small towns and big cities knew these men. These men were in their communities; they were their family, neighbors, and friends. The militiamen comprised most of the forces in Puerto Rico and the Philippines. They had done their part and had the support of the American people.

Ongoing Geographic and Time Constraints

The tradition of the militia being limited to geographic boundaries originated in England when Parliament tried to limit the abuse of the citizen-soldier by the monarch. The early colonial immigrants copied this policy, which hobbled the National Guard's ability to serve as a legitimate reserve force for the regular forces.

The issue was a bureaucratic tangle. If the citizen-soldier wanted to fight in the Spanish-American War (or, later, in World War I), he must resign his position in the state militia and volunteer for federal service. Often, entire militia units volunteered for federal service. However, when the conflicts ended, the "red tape" took over; the federal government had no mechanism to return the militia to their state formations. The practice robbed states of their militia, leaving no one to help confront domestic issues.

Traditional militia laws also limited the time a citizen-soldier could serve at the federal level—militia members had farms and homes to maintain, after all. If their service comprised three months at a time, using them in complex and distant conflicts was difficult, if not impossible. Time limitations were of particular concern in eras when travel was considerably slower. Simply traveling to a warzone could take weeks—a significant chunk of the allotted service time.

Changes: The Dick Acts

After the Civil War, the militia was primarily seen as the strong arm of "robber barons," the business elites who used these men to break up labor disputes. The National Guard leadership and, as time passed, a newly formed lobbying group called the National Guard Association,[10] made a conscious effort to shed their reputation for being a military police force. They wanted to position themselves as a reserve force for the Regular Army.

The National Guard leadership adopted unit structures and uniforms resembling the Regular Army.

During the War of 1812, the militia was used with varying degrees of success. More importantly, the American and British control over the sea lanes illuminated the shortfalls of sharing the responsibility of national defense between the states and federal government. Some governors refused to fill their quotas, and some militiamen showed up ill-trained and fled their positions when attacked.

The independence of each National Guard state was dramatically changed under the 1903 Dick Act (later amended in 1908), which removed the limits on the National Guard's length of service and geographical limitations.

The Dick Act and its amendments created a formal relationship between the state's military forces and the Federal War Department. The act included the needed federal dollars to the states to establish continuity and conformity with the Regular Army. The 1903 law required the Regular Army to inspect the National Guard units and provide training assistance.

The 1908 amendment to the Dick Act dropped any limitation on time the National Guard could be used and stated the National Guard could be used outside the United States.

For the first time, a national call-up was no longer discretionary. A National Guard soldier not reporting for federal service could be subject to court-martial.

---

10   The National Guard Association of the United States (NGAUS) was formed in Washington, DC in 1878 as the Guard's advocate, lobbying for National Guard issues. It remains active to this day.

The Dick Act also created the Division of the Militia Affairs, the predecessor to the National Guard Bureau.

However, in 1908, the Dick Act was deemed unconstitutional. In 1912, Attorney General George W. Wickersham found the use of the National Guard on foreign soil was unconstitutional unless there was actual warfare. The decision devastated the use of the National Guard as a reserve force for the standing Army. The decision created more division between the camps advocating for and against the National Guard as a viable combat reserve force.

National Guard use beyond the Constitution was forbidden by the US Government.

As the two camps could not compromise, Congress created a military composed of the Regular Army, Army Guardsmen, and Army Reservists. The revamped military would be large enough to take on an enemy in Europe.

The National Defense Act of 1916 tried to remedy the problems with National Guard deployments overseas. National Guardsmen would be drafted as individuals into federal service during times of national emergencies. The individuals would then serve in their state-designated units as part of the Regular Army. The states would give up some control over their National Guards to receive more federal funding. The Secretary of War could hold funding from states not following federal regulations.

The Act was a compromise for those who wanted a strong federal military and those who wanted more state control over the national defense. The Act of 1916 relied on the standing Army, the National Guard, and the Army of Reserve forces that would have the ability, if needed, to fight in Europe. The term "National Guard" became the official title for all state militia forces.

In 1916, the National Guard was officially named to bolster our military.

Summary

This chapter discussed how the seeds of the modern National Guard were planted in the tradition of the citizen-soldier in Athens and the colonial militia. The demand came from citizens prepared to confront the threats to the well-being of their communities. The legacy of a part-time warrior living in and serving the community exists today in the National Guard.

The Constitution established the federal system of government with checks and balances. However, the militia defense required cooperation and coordination between the states and the federal government. Congress quickly realized the weakness in the militia defense system. At the time, Congress faced a militia dilemma: states' rights versus national aims.

Congress passed acts that would provide more militia funding and required the states to standardize their training and formations. The Regular Army would provide oversight on the state militias. As a result, the state governor's ability to obstruct or check on the executive was diminished.

Today, it seems relevant for each citizen to ask themselves a philosophical question about their moral obligation to their community. How can they serve?

In the next chapter, we'll look at the evolution of the National Guard through the 20th century and see how the major conflicts forced changes, improvements, and ways of rethinking this essential military branch.

CHAPTER 3

❧

The National Guard in the 20th Century[11]

This chapter continues the evolution of the National Guard in the 20th century, beginning with the Guard's involvement in both World Wars and ending with the procrastination of the Pentagon using the National Guard "roundout" maneuver brigades in Desert Storm. The roundout concept means that a National Guard maneuver brigade is assigned to a two-brigade Active-Duty division, forming a three-brigade division; this crucial support brings the divisions up to full strength when mobilized.

In the 20th century, transportation and technology made the world smaller; journeys that used to take weeks could now be completed in a day, while communication around the globe vastly improved and increased in speed. Our nation's population snowballed, as did its presence on the world stage. The United States became a world power, and our military had to back up that power.

The Guard was in high demand as World War I broke out in Europe.

World War I

Woodrow Wilson used the National Defense Act of 1916 and the Selective Service Act to draft the Guardsmen into Federal service. The Guard could now serve overseas and without time constraints. Their

---

11 For many of the dates, events, and statistics listed in this chapter, I relied on the following book: Doubler, Michael D. *I Am the Guard: A History of the Army National Guard.* Diane Publishing, 2001.
Unless otherwise cited, Mr. Doubler's work served as my resource for information.

connection to their states was severed; their Commander-in-Chief was now the president.

The Selective Service Act of 1917 ended the states' quota system for a more manageable draft, prohibited enlistment bounties, and eliminated hiring substitutes. However, because the United States could not afford to crash its industry machine, the 1917 Selective Service Act also created deferments for men working essential jobs.

The Guard's roots in the community and chances of being drafted increased the volunteers in the National Guard. The local commanders pointed out that joining the Guard would allow men to serve with friends and families from their communities rather than going overseas with strangers and draftees.

Nearly 2.5 million men served in the National Guard during World War I, with over 400,000 Guardsmen mobilized for active duty. Over 42,000 died in battle. The Guardsmen tried to keep their local and state identity with mixed results.

In 1918, the Army issued General Order No. 73. The order stated there was only one Army. Therefore, there would be no distinction between Regulars, Reservists, Guardsmen, and draftees. The Guard was ordered to remove distinctive State or National Guard markings. However, the Guard established Guard Division patches to be worn on their left arm. This provided the Guardsmen an opportunity to display their local and state pride. For example, the 26th Division, with its roots in New England, adopted a shoulder patch that contained the letters Y and D for the Yankee Division.

These Guardsmen proved that, with proper training and equipment, they were a force equal to the Regular Army. Imagine the morale boost to the American people, knowing the men from their cities and states contributed to the additional 400,000 Guard soldiers fighting in Europe. They knew their local guys were in the fight!

The German High Command considered six National Guard divisions among the top eight divisions in the American Army.

The National Guard distinguished itself by its service. One of the most notable regiments came from the streets of Harlem and other New York City neighborhoods. The African American National Guardsmen of the 15th New York Infantry Regiment became the 369th Infantry Regiment.[12] The regiment was mostly comprised of African Americans but also included soldiers from Canada, Cuba, Guyana, Liberia, Portugal, and Puerto Rico, as well as White American officers. Once deployed, they were assigned to support the French army. They went into the infamous trenches of World War I as part of the French 16th Division and served more time in those trenches—a reported 191 days—than any other US unit.

In the aftermath of the war, the 1920s expansion of the National Defense Act offered new legislation that addressed Guardsmen released from active federal duty; they could return to their states in a traditional National Guard status, picking up their lives and duties where they had left off.

The act confirmed the Guard was a vital part of the Army when ordered to federal service. However, the act did not address a sustained relationship between the Regular Army and the Guard during peacetime. The Guard activists were concerned the War Department would leave the National Guard defunct during peace.

Interim

In the years between the two world wars, the National Guard Association of the United States (NGAUS) and its legislative allies pressured Congress for new legislation to protect the Guard's link to the states and sustain its permanent reserve status to the Regular Army. Thus, another amendment to the 1916 National Defense Act was introduced in 1933. Through this amendment, the Guard was declared to always be part of the Army and thus could be ordered into active federal service by the president during a national emergency.

---

12 Harlem Hellfighters citations: *New York Heritage Digital Collections.* "15th New York National Guard Enlistment Records." The New York State Military Museum and Veterans Research Center, https://nyheritage.org/collections/15th-new-york-national-guard-enlistment-records. Trickey, Erick. "One Hundred Years Ago, the Harlem Hellfighters Bravely Led the U.S. Into WWI." *Smithsonian Magazine,* 14 May 2018, https://www.smithsonianmag.com/history/one-hundred-years-ago-harlem-hellfighters-bravely-led-us-wwi-180968977/.

The Guard could also receive a federal mission without a call by state governors.

While the Guard's origin was based on the local militia, the 1933 amendment dramatically changed the trajectory of the Guard's future. The new amendment confirmed the National Guard as a reserve for the Regular Army. The amendment came with increased federal funding and control.

The National Guard remained under the militia clause of the Constitution, but more importantly, it was part of the Army clause of the Constitution. The 1933 act joined the two clauses together under the law. This act was critical in supporting the dual-status mission of the National Guard. The Guard would officially have two masters but train for federal wartime missions.

World War II

In 1939, the Second World War broke out overseas and threatened the United States. By August 1940, Franklin D. Roosevelt ordered the Guard into active service, which bolstered the federal service with more than 300,000 men in 18 combat divisions and nearly 5,000 men from 29 National Guard observation squadrons. This undoubtedly doubled the strength of the Army instantly.

The Guard participated in 34 separate campaigns across the Second World War. The 29th Division, with units in Virginia, Maryland, and the District of Columbia, participated in the Normandy D-Day landings in 1944.

The 37th Ohio National Guard "Buckeyes" Division took part in the assault to drive Japanese forces out of Manila. It was treacherous fighting. The Japanese had fortified buildings, and the 37th found themselves fighting block-by-block, floor-by-floor, and room-by-room.

148 presidential citations were awarded to National Guard units for outstanding performance of duty or conspicuous valor or heroism. Individual Guardsmen received 20 Medals of Honor, 50 Distinguished Service Crosses, 48 Distinguished Flying Crosses, and over 500 Silver Star Medals.

The Guardsmen units were demobilized post-war. Personnel returned to civilian life. The surge capability of the National Guard proved itself in both World Wars, but obviously, the story is far from over. With the onset of the Korean War, the Guard's existence and purpose were renewed.

Korean War (1950 - 1953)

The Korean War was a devastating conflict that lasted for three years and killed millions of people. However, the National Guard played a key role in the war, with six divisions vitally important in the conflict. These divisions were able to provide support to troops on the ground, helping to achieve victory over the enemy.

The first National Guard division to arrive on the scene was the 40th Infantry Division, comprised of units from the Western United States, which landed in Korea in July 1950. This unit provided support and stability during the initial stages of the conflict, helping to keep North Korean forces from advancing further into South Korea. The 40th Infantry Division continued playing a crucial role in the conflict, helping to repel the Chinese forces that attacked the UN lines in May 1951. This unit could use its heavy weapons and artillery fire to keep the enemy at bay while other South Korean units moved into position.

National Guard units weren't just in combat operations. The Guard set up base camps, supplied food and ammunition to the troops, assisted with medical care, and provided transportation. They offered essential support for the troops by building airstrips, communications networks, bridges, roads, and other infrastructure.

The 45th Infantry Division, primarily comprised of units from Oklahoma, arrived in October 1952 and became the first National Guard division to stay in Korea for an extended period. This unit provided a much-needed presence on the ground and was able to fight along with South Korean forces in the Battle of Triangle Hill, in which the Allies defeated Chinese forces.

Titles 10 and 32, Post-Korean War

After the Korean War, important legislation was passed. In 1956, Congress created Title 10, US Code, which pertained to all federal military forces, including the National Guard in a federal status. This title is the full-time regular military; the National Guard is included when they are federalized. The soldiers are paid with federal funds, and the president is the Commander-in-Chief.

The National Guard soldiers are under Title 10 (federal authority) when they deploy for combat overseas. They are under the Uniform Code of Military Justice (UCMJ). When the National Guard is on a Title 10 status, the scope of their use domestically is limited because they then fall under the Posse Comitatus Act[13].

That same year, Congress passed Title 32, a US Code that consolidated all the laws regarding the National Guard. This is the normal status of the National Guard soldiers when they are drilling and training on the weekends. The soldiers fall under the control of the governor of the state and the state military code of military justice. Under Title 32, the Guard does not fall under Posse Comitatus. The soldier in this status can be used for domestic operations. However, the federal government provides the funding to cover the pay of Guardsmen on Title 32 status.

The Regular Army and the part-time force of the Reserve are only Title 10 forces. The National Guard's uniqueness is that it can be paid with federal funds in Title 10 and Title 32 status.

Finally, the National Guard can fall under State Active Duty (SAD). In this case, the soldier is under the command of the governor and paid from their respective state coffers, normally to support civilian operations. The pay and benefits vary from state to state. The National Guard soldiers in this status do not fall under Posse Comitatus.

The status of the National Guard Soldier is vital for the scope of support for domestic operations. This will be discussed in further chapters.

Furthermore, the 1956 law required members of both the Reserve and National Guard to attend basic training at active-duty installations. This allowed units to receive collective training starting at the squad level.

---

13   The Posse Comitatus Act (1878) declares that federal troops cannot participate in civilian law enforcement unless authorized to do so by law.

The paid drills were updated, along with providing meals, which were made available for soldiers on eight-hour drill periods. Drills also moved to the weekends. As Army National Guard units were a critical part of the Army's Strategic Reserve Force (STRAF), the training plans were focused on possible deployments.

The Berlin Crisis

The fallout of World War II resulted in a divided Berlin—a division that grew worse as the Cold War initiated and became quite literal in 1961. That year, the Soviet Union built a wall that separated the city of East Berlin from the West.

To address the crisis, Congress passed a joint resolution authorizing the federalization of 250,000 Guardsmen for 12 months to deter further Soviet aggression. Some units backfilled the active-duty Army while two divisions were identified for an overseas mission. The active Army inspectors declared the two Guard divisions combat-ready four months after mobilization. This marked the first time in history that a reserve force was mobilized as a political instrument to deter war.

The Vietnam War (1955 - 1975)

When President Johnson inherited the American involvement in Vietnam, he was determined not to give the communists an easy victory. In 1964, Congress gave the president authority in the Gulf of Tonkin Resolution "to take all necessary steps, including the use of armed force" to defend South Vietnam.[14]

For the most part, President Johnson refused to mobilize the National Guard and the Reserves. He believed activating the Reserve forces would provoke China and Russia into a larger war in Southeast Asia. He opted not to disrupt American society with a major mobilization and community involvement, unlike in World War I and II. He ignored the cost-benefits of using an already trained National Guard force for a draft. More importantly, President Johnson undermined the value the citizen-soldier brings to foreign wars.

---

14   Doubler, M. *I Am the Guard: A History of the Army National Guard.* Diane Publishing, 2001, p. 223.

The Vietnam War was largely fought with Regular Forces augmented with draftees. The history of draft loopholes goes back to militia mandatory service. The colonial governments normally provided clergy, high-ranking government officials, university students, tradesmen, and fishermen exemptions from service.[15] During the Vietnam War, the National Guard became a loophole for men to skirt the draft and avoid service in an unpopular war.

As the war dragged on, more men signed up for the Guard. The capacity was at its peak, and a strength ceiling was imposed in 1968 of 400,000.[16]

In 1968, out of desperation, the president issued an executive order that activated 24,500 Guard and Reserves. Altogether, about 9,000 Guardsmen served in Vietnam as individuals or in a unit.[17]

While most Guard units did not deploy to Vietnam, the ones that did reinforced the reputation of citizen-soldiers performing very well in combat.

On April 19, 1968, the 2nd Battalion 138th Field Artillery unit from the Kentucky National Guard was ordered to active duty. Like most National Guard battalions, the 138th Battalion had units in several towns, including Louisville, Bardstown, Elizabethtown, and Carrollton. In total, about 570 men were deployed to Vietnam from the battalion. In this battalion, there were numerous pairs of brothers serving in combat together. The battalion provided fire support to the active-duty units on several fire bases. The Kentucky citizen-soldiers were so successful in providing fire support that the North Vietnam army sappers were ordered to destroy the Charlie Battery of Bardstown, Kentucky, at Fire Base Tomahawk.

On June 19, 1969, about 150 Viet Cong sappers launched a massive attack against the American Fire Base Tomahawk. The Viet Cong overran the base security and attempted to destroy everything. Despite a vicious sneak attack involving killing the noble infantrymen on guard at the perimeter and causing extensive damage to the structures of the

15   Ibid., p. 27
16   Ibid., p. 224
17   Ibid., p. 226

base, the enemy was unable to succeed in their mission. The determined fight of the Guardsmen—many of whom were wounded—forced the enemy into retreat. Citizens in Bardstown also had thirteen of their men killed or wounded in action from the attack.

General Creighton Abrams, the Senior Commander in Vietnam, said the 2nd Battalion 138th Field Artillery was "one of the best trained, and absolutely the best maintained battalion-sized units in Vietnam."[18]

During the war, Army leaders took note of the camaraderie, enthusiasm, and maturity of the Guardsmen over the draftees. The Vietnam War convinced Army Chief of Staff General Abrams that America should never again go to war without the full support of the American people.

The Pentagon announced the Total Force Policy, which would further integrate the Regular Army with the National Guard and Reserves.

The Gates Commission ended the draft and moved the country into an all-volunteer era. The Guard had to hone their recruitment skills once again. By the 1970s, active efforts were made to recruit women and minorities.

Vietnam was not a decisive victory for America. The war dragged on without the support of the American people. The roundout brigades were created, to permanently link the National Guard brigades to an active-duty Army division. A National Guard brigade made one of the Regular Army brigades in their division. In theory, this would cement the American people's involvement in future conflicts. The National Guard roundout brigade would deploy and fight with the active Army division.

President Johnson created a new paradigm for limited wars. He purposely distanced the American people from the conflict in Vietnam. Not only was the Vietnam War a crushing loss for the regular Army and draftees, but it established a lasting impression of the National Guard on the American people. The pride in their hometown heroes who had served in both World Wars and the Korean War had been squandered.

---

18   Resource information and further details on this fascinating story of heroism can be found at: *Ky.gov.* "The Vietnam War." Kentucky National Guard eMuseum, https://kynghistory.ky.gov/Our-History/History-of-the-Guard/Pages/The-Vietnam-War.aspx.

American culture lost the understanding of the Guard's selfless service in combat. What remained was confusion over the Guard's role.

President Johnson's decision not to mobilize Reserve forces for most of the Vietnam War left an unpleasant legacy on the Guard and its reputation. Cuts in military spending and the end of the draft weakened the entire military system.

Desert Storm – 1991

President George H.W. Bush used the 1976 mobilization authority in Section 673b, Title 10, US Code, which authorized the mobilization of 200,000 Reserve forces. Both the Regular Army and Army National Guard implemented the "Stop Loss" policy that prevented soldiers from voluntarily leaving service.

While the president wanted to mobilize the Reserves, Secretary of Defense Dick Cheney specified that the Guard could only provide combat support and support units. Combat units did not have the authority to mobilize.

As a result, the active-duty divisions deployed without a National Guard roundout brigade. The failure of the Pentagon to deploy the National Guard's roundout brigades stirred a rift between Regular Army and National Guard forces and a demand for answers by Congress.

In November, President Bush signed another executive order authorizing the mobilization of Guard and Reserve combat units for the possible use of the ground offensive in Kuwait.

The National Guard provided 62,411 soldiers to the Persian Gulf in 398 units. Most units left the United States within 20 days of being called up and two-thirds within 45 days.

However, without the roundout brigades, Desert Storm was fought without any National Guard maneuver units.

Summary

The 20th century saw the rise of the American hegemon and a new world order. The need for a reliable and capable military escalated. The evolution from the colonial militia to a modern National Guard was basically complete. The dual status of the National Guard as both a state and federal asset was confirmed.

After the wars, the Guardsmen returned home to receive the support of their local people and reestablished their civilian lives. The soldiers who trained in their local armories, considered hometown heroes, brought the wars to the American people. Not only were the soldiers and families sacrificing for the wars, but so were the local businesses and employers.

Despite the obvious financial benefits, community ties, and success in World War I and II, and the Korean War, the use of the Guard was still questioned in the 20th century.

The war in Vietnam was not only a low point for the Regular Army but for the National Guard as well. President Johnson decided to draft men and leave the Guard largely at home. This action during an unpopular war left a lasting stigma and confusion about the Guard in the minds of the American people.

Desert Storm saw the Pentagon leaving the roundout National Guard brigades at home. The reason for their decision is likely rooted in the inherent tensions in the American system and the fight for resources and relevance. The tensions inherent in our American federal system are discussed in the next chapter.

CHAPTER 4

State and Federal Tensions

The National Guard has repeatedly deployed to face the most severe crises on American soil. Occasionally, over the decades, tensions flared over "federal control" versus "state sovereignty." Governors used the Guard in ways that did not always sit well with the representatives in Washington and vice versa.

How it began

The seeds of political conflict over militia control originated with the Founding Fathers, who were split between two ideologies. The Federalists, led by Alexander Hamilton, wanted a strong central government with a standing Army for national defense. On the other hand, the Anti-Federalists (a.k.a. the Democratic-Republican Party), led by Thomas Jefferson and James Madison, favored more state power with a militia-based national defense.

Their first debates concerned the ratification of the Constitution. They compromised on a government structure with distributed power between the states and the central government. Surprisingly, the original intent of the Anti-Federalists was for the state militias to provide a check-and-balance system against any tyrannical central authority.

The National Guard's dual nature of serving both the president and a state's governor has put the Guard at the center of multiple political debates.

As we have clearly seen, the Guard's dual mission was a process of evolution. The citizen-soldier serves both the governor and the president of the United States, though that service was never simultaneous. The Guard's obligation is always transferred back and forth between the two.

At times, the governor's control over the National Guard has placed the president's foreign policy in jeopardy. In these situations, the National Guard was used as a political tool between a governor and the president.

This happened in the war in 1812.

Governors Refuse the War of 1812

This war against Great Britain highlighted the problems with the militia, namely that it was controlled by governors of states who had their political self-interests. Nevertheless, the Constitution established the militia to "provide for the common defense" of the United States.

The Governors in New England, who depended on sea trade with England, were against the war. Governor John C. Smith of Connecticut questioned the constitutionality of the war, stating that "Britain's challenges at sea are not an invasion." To his thinking, there was no need to enforce the laws or suppress insurrections, and he asserted that President Madison's call for the militia was outside his presidential authority.[19]

After two years, the states protesting the use of their militia for this war finally agreed to place them in federal service, with the stipulation that the militia be used only to protect their coastline.[20]

Therefore, while the constitutional plan for the militia was to provide for national security, this plan relied on the skills of the president to convince and align the cooperation of the states and their governors. The War of 1812 demonstrated the inherent political limitations involved. Simply put, what happened when those governors refused to cooperate?

---

19 Doubler, M. *I Am the Guard: A History of the Army National Guard.* Diane Publishing, 2001, p. 79.
20 Ibid.

Political disagreements between governors and presidents would continue to undermine not only the ability of the federal government to engage in foreign wars but also domestic policy.

States' Rights and the Civil War

The Civil War was a crisis of the federal system. The Southern States' political motivations conflicted directly with those of the newly elected president.

When President Lincoln was elected, the Southern States believed their right to own slaves would be compromised. Those states began to secede from the Union in defiance of Lincoln.

President Lincoln invoked the Calling Forth Act in 1861 and called 75,000 militiamen into federal service for ninety days to end the insurrection.[21]

Northern governors cooperated with President Lincoln and furnished militia units to support the Union Army. However, certain states sympathetic to the Confederacy, even those that never seceded from the Union, refused to contribute militia. Governor Beriah Magoffin, the governor of Kentucky, was the first to refuse to send his required quota. He stated, "No troops for the wicked purpose of subduing [Kentucky's] sister Southern states."[22]

Posse Comitatus

After the Civil War, the Southern governors were left in office under the Presidential Reconstruction Plan. Tragically, just when the Thirteenth Amendment abolished slavery, the Ku Klux Klan came into existence. Formed by a group of former Confederates, the Klan immediately waged a campaign of sheer terrorism against freed slaves, among others.

Congress, disturbed by this violent defiance in the South, passed the 1871 Ku Klux Klan Act. Its purpose was to enforce the provisions of the Fourteenth Amendment (which gave citizenship rights and protections

---

21 Ibid, p. 95
22 Ibid.

to any person born in the United States) and to stop abuses and other unjust limitations imposed on the freedom of Black citizens.[23]

Union federal forces were sent to protect the newly freed slaves.[24] Regular Army troops were used at polling places and to enforce the Reconstruction policies.

The Southern leaders argued that using the Union's Federal Army to enforce civilian rule went against the Founding Fathers' intent in the Constitution. They reminded Congress that this country was founded on the strong distaste of the Redcoats in colonial life.

In the next presidential election, Samuel J. Tilden won the popular vote, while Rutherford B. Hayes took the electoral vote. The election was disputed by three Southern states and Oregon.[25] Congress ultimately picked Hayes. Part of the reason for this selection was Hayes's promise to remove Union Federal Forces from the Southern states.

The Posse Comitatus Act was passed in 1878 and expanded to include all active components. However, the law *does not apply to the National Guard when it is under the control of the state governors.* This is why the National Guard can be used to provide security, protection, or deterrence during tense civilian conflicts. The Posse Comitatus Act ensured governors would have the ability to control domestic issues with their National Guard.

In hindsight, we can see that in the beginning, this law was a way to enforce Jim Crow laws in the South and disregard federal laws, protecting the status quo of Southern racism. The law removed the federal forces. Thus, the governors could enforce the laws they wanted with a militia force under their control.

Despite this inauspicious origin, the Act is now an important part of American culture and our military system. It gave governors control of their domestic emergencies and civil disturbances. Because of the Posse Comitatus Act, under most circumstances, the president cannot use the regular military for domestic law enforcement.

---

23 The National Constitution Center. https://constitutioncenter.org/.
24 Dougherty, Candidus. "Necessity Hath No Law: Executive Power and the Posse Comitatus Act." *Campbell Law Review*, 2008, p. 12.
25 Ibid., p. 14.

However, according to the Insurrection Act of 1807, the president may override the Posse Comitatus Act and deploy the US military and the National Guard in the United States under circumstances of civil disorder, insurrection, or rebellion.

Segregation

In 1956, Tennessee Governor Frank G. Clement used the National Guard to support integration. The Guard protected Black students against the Ku Klux Klan and other anti-integration protestors in Clinton, Tennessee. The overwhelming show of force allowed a group of African American children to attend school.[26] The Kentucky governor did the same thing with minimal violence.

Unfortunately, this was not the case in every situation of desegregation. Since the founding of the country to current times, governors have periodically disagreed with the politics of the president.

This was the case in Little Rock.

Little Rock Crisis

The National Guard was at the center of a constitutional crisis in Little Rock, Arkansas, in 1957. Five years earlier, the Supreme Court ruled on *Brown vs. The Board of Education* in Topeka. The 1952 decision reversed the 1896 Court decision in *Plessy v. Ferguson* that upheld segregation based on race.

In Little Rock, the school board opted to comply with the Court's decision. They planned to allow nine Black children to attend Little Rock Central High School.

However, Arkansas Governor Orval Faubus wanted no part of this plan. He stated that desegregation of schools was unconstitutional and that integrating the school system in Arkansas would lead to violence.[27] He disregarded the Court's decision, using the Arkansas National Guard to support his political beliefs. The citizen-soldiers were called out to prevent the nine students from entering the high school. As White mobs formed and rioted to prevent the Black students from attending,

---

26 Ibid, p. 213.
27 Ibid., p. 214.

Governor Faubus declared the citizen-soldiers were there to provide peace and stability.

Meanwhile, the United States watched a state governor defy a Supreme Court decision with the Arkansas militia. Even worse, the world watched as the United States defended discrimination.

The mayor of Little Rock sent two telegrams to President Eisenhower requesting federal troops to stabilize the situation.

It is important to remember that the Cold War between the Soviet Union and the United States still dominated foreign policy at this time. President Eisenhower had a crisis on his hands. Faced with a governor directly disobeying a Supreme Court decision, he also knew the USSR would leverage these obvious civil rights inequalities against the United States on the global stage—and the United States could not afford to lose any ground in the Cold War.

Eisenhower made the difficult decision to use federal troops on American citizens. He issued Executive Order 10730, which federalized the entire Arkansas National Guard, returning them to their armories and removing them from Governor Faubus's control. Eisenhower then sent in elements of the 101st Airborne Division. President Eisenhower's action of using federal troops as enforcement on American soil had not been seen since the Reconstruction era following the Civil War.

Later, the Arkansas National Guard resumed protection duties, taking over for the 101st Airborne Division.

Alabama 1963

In 1963, Governor George Wallace of Alabama activated seven hundred Guardsmen. Their mission was to "maintain law and order" at the University of Tuscaloosa. He intended to block African Americans from enrolling in the university. Governor Wallace personally stood in front of the doors and prevented the students from entering.[28]

President John F. Kennedy issued Executive Order 11111, federalizing the entire National Guard to assist the Department of Justice in maintaining the peace and enforcing the law. The federal officials and

---

28   Ibid.

African-American students were escorted to campus with members of the Alabama National Guard, who carried rifles and fixed bayonets.

Imagine the position of the National Guard soldiers during these times. They lived in these communities, often knew the people involved, and may have held political beliefs that didn't align with their orders. Nevertheless, they did their duty and served the governor and president in turn.

Soldiers in a situation like this, being pushed from side to side by opposing opinions, must undoubtedly exist in a strange limbo. One week, they are serving one side of a cause; the following week, their leadership has changed, as well as their side of the fight. The National Guard can usually find peace with their role by remembering that, in effect, their duty is to ensure public safety, regardless of the politics of the situation. But the ability for a president to remove control of the National Guard from a governor does mean that a state's Guard is an obvious pawn to play in political maneuvers.

Throughout the United States, due to the Civil Rights movement, the 1960s were a time of numerous tense gatherings that often erupted into violent riots. The National Guard, in domestic operations, became critical to governors.

Secretary of Defense McNamara reduced the size of the National Guard infrastructure in 1967. The governors argued successfully for enough military police, medical, aviation, and logistical units to provide civil support to their states.[29]

The Guard Under President Ronald Reagan

Under President Ronald Reagan's administration in the 1980s, the National Guard again became a significant tool in political powerplays. The Iran-Contra scandal placed Reagan under Congressional scrutiny for his alleged involvement in illegally providing funds and training to Contra militias. At the same time, under his command, National Guard personnel were sent to train in South America.

Though the soldiers were doing humanitarian training, twelve governors opposed the administration's use of their Guardsmen in South America.

---

29   Ibid., p. 222

The Armed Forces Reserve Act of 1952 gave governors the ability to approve or turn down National Guard training outside the US. Thus, in 1986, the governors began challenging the president's authority to send National Guard troops to South America for training.

In 1986, Representative Montgomery proposed the Montgomery Amendment, which reduced the veto ability of governors. Governor Perpich challenged the law with five other states in 1986. In 1990, the Supreme Court upheld that Congress may authorize the National Guard to active duty for training outside the United States without the consent of the governors or a declaration of a national emergency.

National Guard Deployments

In July 2005, governors expressed concern about the Guard's use in Iraq and Afghanistan. At that time, Guard troops represented 40% of the US ground forces in Iraq. For example, 44% percent of the Montana Guard members were mobilized, Hawaii had 50% mobilized, and Idaho had 46% of their Guardsman activated. In July 2005, the average for a state or territory was 20% of their Guard force deployed.[30] Governors relied on the Guard to help with hurricanes, earthquakes, riots, and other disasters or unexpected events. With large numbers of their Guard federalized and sent away, states were left in uncertain and potentially dangerous circumstances.

Governor Schweitzer from Montana requested the Pentagon return some of his Guard members during the heart of the wildfire season in July and August. The Governor said the Pentagon ignored his request and increased the demand for state units. He stated the Pentagon was not listening to the legitimate requests and needs of the states.

One month later, Hurricane Katrina hit Louisiana. At the time, 40% of Louisiana's National Guard was deployed in Iraq. Critics claim using the National Guard to boost troop numbers left the state vulnerable.[31]

---

30   Associated Press. "Governors Concerned About National Guard Troops." *LA Times Archives*, 17 Jul. 2005, www.latimes.com/archives/la-xpm-2005-jul-17-na-governors17-story.html.

31   *HandWiki.* "Philosophy: Criticism of government response to Hurricane Katrina." Philosophy Portal, https://handwiki.org/wiki/Philosophy:Criticism_of_government_response_to_Hurricane_Katrina.

Hurricane Katrina

The 2005 response to Hurricane Katrina at local, state, and federal levels lagged while people suffered. When it came to accountability, the leadership at all levels pointed fingers.

Governor Kathleen Blanco ordered her National Guard to State Active Duty (SAD) and requested a state of emergency from President George Bush in August 2005. She asked for additional National Guard support from other states via a letter to the National Guard Bureau.

The Joint Task Force from Northern Command, Active Duty, asked the Governor to give up control of her National Guard to the Joint Task Force in September. The Governor refused, rejecting the offer of allowing Louisiana National Guardsmen to command federal and state forces. She feared losing control of the Guard. The Governor testified to Congress that she felt pressure from the White House to federalize the National Guard. She believed the pressure was not purely military but political. She said it was "posturing instead of a real solution."[32] In time, the National Guard soldiers were operating under Title 32, funded by the federal government but allowed states to maintain command and control. Considering the difficulties faced by her state, the Governor's desire to remain in control is understandable.

Over two-weeks in September, 3,700 Guardsman from the 256th Brigade Combat Team redeployed back to Louisiana. The Guardsmen were just back from Iraq, some had experienced roadside bombs, suicide bombers, and the loss of their fellow Guardsmen. Suddenly, they were on patrol with loaded M16s in the disaster zone that was New Orleans. This extremely stressful situation had the potential for violence, as considerable looting took place among the remaining residents of New Orleans (though, in many cases, these were people searching for essential supplies that were not otherwise available).

As a result of the disaster, the National Defense Act of 2007 extended the president's authority during domestic emergencies. The Guard could be federalized if the president determined that the authorities in

---

32 *GovInfo.gov.* "Hurricane Katrina: The Defense Department's role in the response." Senate Hearing 109-813, 9 Feb. 2006, https://www.govinfo.gov/content/pkg/CHRG-109shrg27028/html/CHRG-109shrg27028.htm.

a state were incapable of maintaining public order.[33] This law created a political storm. Each state and territorial governor joined together to demand a repeal of the amendment.

The Guard Under President Donald Trump

The Washington, DC National Guard acts like all other National Guards, except the president is the Commander in Chief. In that way, it is unique. An executive order in 1969 delegated the command of the DC National Guard to the secretary of defense, but the president still has the discretion to call out the guard.[34]

In 2020, in response to protests regarding the killing of George Floyd, President Trump deployed the DC National Guard, over the objections of the DC mayor, ostensibly to keep the peace in DC, even though these protests had shown few signs of violence. The political controversy over the authority of this decision became heated. Meanwhile, eleven other state governors deployed their Guard soldiers to DC to protect monuments (though it is debated whether they were dispatched to shore up the smaller DC Guard). The soldiers were on Title 32 status. In theory, soldiers from various states were supposed to be under the control of their governors, but they were reporting up through the DC Guard's chain of command directly to President Trump.[35]

It appeared the Guard was reporting to a federal chain of command on Title 32 status. Therefore, the National Guard was used once again as a pawn in the middle of a significant philosophical and political disruption.

Border Crisis

In 2018, President Trump sent members of the National Guard to support US Customs and Border Protection.

---

33 Sausville, P. "DOD Response to Natural Disasters—Why the National Guard is Off Limits." US Army War College, 2008.

34 *Congress.gov.* "The National Guard and the COVID-19 Pandemic Response." Congressional Research Service, 12 Mar. 2021, https://crsreports.congress.gov/product/pdf/IF/IF11483.

35 Anderson, Scott R. et al. "What Made Trump's Protest Response in D.C. Unique?" *Lawfare,* 8 Jun. 2020, https://www.lawfareblog.com/what-made-trumps-protest-response-dc-unique.

In 2021, South Dakota Governor Kristi Noem used private donations to fund the deployment of 48 South Dakota National Guardsmen to the US and Mexico Border. She was responding to Texas Governor Greg Abbott's plea for help to augment border security. The Governor publicly criticized President Biden's border security as being weak.

The South Dakota Guardsmen were on State Active Duty orders, and Governor Noem was their Commander in Chief. In other words, no federal funds or authority applied to this mission.

The controversy was unprecedented. Some criticized the situation as unethical, presenting the National Guard as available to the highest bidder and, therefore, no better than mercenaries.[36] Others said the situation risked politicizing the military.

The governors stated undocumented immigrants were breaking local and federal laws while there was almost no security at the border.

The 2022 National Defense Act blocked governors from doing this in the future, prohibiting private funding for interstate deployment of the National Guard.

Operation Lone Star

In March 2021, Governor Greg Abbott launched Operation Lone Star to use the Texas National Guard and the Department of Public Safety (DPS) at his state's border. The Texas Governor accused the Biden administration of inaction and allowing drug smuggling and illegal immigration. At the time of this writing, about 10,000 members of the Texas Military Department are assigned to Operation Lone Star. The Texas Guardsmen are being paid out of the state coffers in a State Active Duty status. The Governor of Texas is the Commander in Chief.

In October 2022, the secretary of the Department of Homeland Security requested help from the DOD. At that time, the defense secretary approved the deployment of 2,500 National Guardsmen to the border.

---

36   Horton, Alex. "South Dakota governor sending National Guard to Mexico border on mission funded by GOP megadonor." *The Washington Post*, 29 Jun. 2021, https://www.washingtonpost.com/national-security/2021/06/29/south-dakota-national-guard-texas-border/.

In May 2023, President Biden temporarily surge 1,500 active-duty military members to the southern border for 90 days. The full-time federal forces will help with administrative and logistical support, not law enforcement. The decision coincides with the expiration of Title 42,[37] a policy that restricted individuals from crossing the border to seek asylum during the COVID-19 era.[38]

The military and National Guard on the southern border will likely be a political battlefield for years to come.

COVID-19 Vaccination Controversy

On August 24, 2021, Secretary of Defense Lloyd Austin directed the US military, including the National Guard, to get the COVID-19 vaccine. Austin followed with a memo that stated non-compliant people would not be paid or allowed to participate in drills or other training and risked being kicked out of the military.

Oklahoma, Texas, and Alaska governors all filed lawsuits to challenge the Department of Defense vaccine policy. These governors cited President Biden's overreach and the impact on their National Guard strength if their soldiers were removed from service.

Governor Greg Abbott's lawsuit stated that the federal government has no command authority over the Guardsmen serving the state on Title 32. The case challenges the federal government's unconstitutional action to force Texas to submit to federal orders and impose federally dictated action on Guardsmen when they are not federalized (Title 10). The heart of the case is state sovereignty.[39]

---

37 Thomas, Steff Danielle. "Biden defends decision to send troops to the border: 'They need more people to clear people.'" *The Hill,* 5 May 2023, https://thehill.com/homenews/administration/3991312-biden-defends-decision-to-send-troops-to-the-border-they-need-more-people-to-clear-people/.

38 Bertrand, Natasha, Priscilla Alvarez, and Haley Britzky. "Biden admin to send 1,500 troops to southern border for support roles ahead of expected migrant surge." *CNN,* 2 May 2023, https://www.cnn.com/2023/05/02/politics/us-troops-border-migrant-surge/index.html.

39 *SupremeCourt.gov.* "Biden et al. V. Texas et al." Supreme Court of the United States Slip Opinion, 30 Jun. 2022, https://www.supremecourt.gov/opinions/21pdf/21-954_7l48.pdf.

In a November 2022 letter to Congress, Governor Bill Lee of Tennessee said the COVID-19 mandate created a significant problem. The National Guard missed its recruiting target by 10%, and 7,500 members left the service. The National Guard was preparing to discharge approximately 14,000 soldiers over the next two years because they refused the COVID-19 vaccine. He stated the governor's ability to respond to natural disasters and emergencies is contingent upon the strength and size of the National Guard.[40] He called upon Congress to immediately remove President Biden's administration's COVID-19 vaccine mandate.

The 2023 National Defense Authorization Act (NDAA) required the Department of Defense to rescind the vaccine mandate. However, as of May 2023, the determination of what to do with the National Guard members negatively impacted by the mandatory COVID-19 vaccination policy has yet to be determined.

Summary

The American National Guard has participated in every American war on the front lines. Still, it has also been called upon to address domestic disputes as the country has transformed culturally, economically, and politically. During these times, individual National Guardsman values and beliefs have been tested too.

The 1957 Little Rock, Arkansas desegregation situation is a direct result of the American federal system the Framers of the Constitution created. The Constitution establishes a separation of powers between the states and the federal government. In the middle of the federal system is the National Guard.

The Framers built a militia system controlled by the states but included provisions allowing the federal government to employ them. The state control of the militia was seen as a check on the federal government to prevent too much military power. However, as time went on, the states' ability to counter the federal government was reduced.

---

40 WPLN. "Gov. Lee appeals to Congress to end COVID vaccine mandate affecting 800 Tennessee guardsman.", 01 Dec 200, https://wpln.org/post/gov-lee-appeals-to-congress-to-end-covid-vaccine-mandate-affecting-800-tennessee-guardsmen/.

Through the years, the control over the National Guard has been tested. The tests included governors' resistance to federal control based on political differences, such as in Little Rock in 1957.

The National Guard has been sent to our southern border. We've sent them across the country during the COVID-19 vaccination mandate.

Just recently, we've seen unprecedented politicization of the Guard. They were active during Black Lives Matter protests during President Trump and President Biden's administrations. This appears to spring from different levels of the federal government.

The conflicts between state and federal control are not the only arena under which the National Guard experiences controversy. In the next chapter, we'll discuss the various tensions that can arise between the Regular Army and the National Guard.

CHAPTER 5

Tensions Between the Regular Army and the National Guard

The inherent tensions between the Regular Army and the National Guard spring from the exact origins as the tensions between federal and state control of the National Guard, the dichotomy that has existed since our country first formed. Do we want a professional military force, or do we want a regular militia?

What happens when we need—and have—both?

As discussed in the previous chapters, the modern-day American Army Total Force comprises three components: the Regular Army, Army Reserve, and Army National Guard. The modern military didn't just appear with one mastermind law—it was an evolution that supported the United States' dominance on the world stage. However, none of the components would exist if it weren't for organizational or congressional champions.

Nevertheless, for the transition of the United States' primary defense organization moving from the state militias to the Regular Army, there had to be political biases toward a federal force and criticisms of the citizen-soldier. The National Guard and its advocates went on the defensive to retain their organization.

This chapter focuses on the tensions between the Regular Component and National Guard. The Federalists had to square an argument for a

Regular Army with the American ideal of liberalism and the fear of a standing Army trampling on the rights of individuals.[41]

As the United States engaged in more wars, the advocates for a professional force had their ammunition. At times, due to the nature of the decentralized force, the militia performed poorly. The common criticism became that the state militias lacked standardization and adequate training.

Since the creation of the Constitution, our system has produced laws that worked around the founding document-camps formed on both sides of the argument.

The early American system raised the military and a permanent citizen-soldier militia as needed. Still, this system was doomed because it required political cooperation between the two levels of government. Whenever the self-interests of states stood in the way of the federal government's objectives, such as in the incidents during the War of 1812, the justification for growing the steady professional force of a Regular Army strengthened. Yet the need for state militias was seldom in doubt.

The military is inherently part of the federal political system, so it depends on Congress for funding. Congressional support for a robust Regular Army and a National Guard has waxed and waned throughout history.

This dynamic changed during the Cold War. Activists on each side aimed to increase their relevance and resources.

Politics equates to the activities associated with decisions and power over the distribution of resources. The people who create our pivotal military policies have often worn the uniform of one side of the debate or the other. George Washington was a militia man during the French and Indian War, then the Commander in Chief of the Continental Army during the Revolutionary War.

Let's look at the champions and adversaries of the National Guard and how they impacted the modern force.

---

41   Tovy, Tal. "Militia or Regular Army?" *Open Edition Journals,* https://journals.openedition. org/ejas/7814.

The Great Divide

We have already noted the two sides of this debate.

Some would prefer a standing Army, who want a federal force that cannot be controlled at a state level. Supporters of a robust standing party pointed to the National Guard's failures in "readiness." People fear that state authority could usurp the federal rule, as in 1812 and 1861, and that it is dangerous to depend on those forces because of their dual allegiance to state and federal missions.[42]

However, those in favor of a National Guard also have strong arguments. These advocates promoted the idea of a smaller standing Army, a larger Army National Guard, and a Army Reserve force.

Both the Greek and Roman citizen-soldiers fought to defend their lands and way of life in their city-states. Early Americans liked the idea of the citizen-soldier returning to his domestic life after the battle. George Mason, a colonial revolutionary, argued that when the Romans maintained the nature of their citizen-soldier militia, their political and social freedoms were sustained with the rise of their empire. Still, when the system was abandoned, the Roman Republic fell. [43]

The American tradition goes back to Great Britain. As a result of their experience with the Red Coats and knowledge of the constant European battles, colonial Americans feared large standing armies because they were viewed as repressive government agents.[44]

The United States was unlike Europe in that there were no neighboring rivals or constant threats of war. The United States was blessed geopolitically with a large ocean between it and Europe and no significant competitors with a stronghold on the continent. The country could be protected with citizen-soldiers, a small Regular Army, and consultatory service.

Of course, the National Guard has a cost-benefit. The Guard only costs a fraction of what the Regular Army does. The Guard's connection to the community and the people is the real benefit.

---

42 Doubler, p. 134
43 Tovy, Tal. "Militia or Regular Army?" *Open Edition Journals,* https://journals.openedition.org/ejas/7814.
44 Doubler, p. 17

John A. Logan

After the Civil War, John A. "Blackjack" Logan (1826-1886) of Illinois was an early outspoken critic of the system dominated by West Point officers.

I'll offer a brief explanation about this West Point matter: It is not so much targeting the military academy itself as it is a concern that all Army officers at the time were being filtered through the same system, leaving no room for diversity in leadership.

Thomas Jefferson was an Anti-Federalist and advocate for the militia. He believed the militia was an "essential principle of our government."[45] However, as President, he mixed his ideals with reality. He created a small Regular Army that would be more professional and have limited self-government values.

In 1802, Congress supported President Jefferson and passed an act that created the US Military Academy at West Point. In response, the states developed military academies, such as Virginia Military Institute and The Citadel in South Carolina.

West Point was founded in 1812. At the time, and after controversial issues with the militia in the War of 1812, the Secretary of War believed the military should plan for war with the Regulars rather than the militia. West Point created a professional and trained group of new officers. They and the other military academies transitioned civilians into Regular Army second lieutenants. At the time, no additional military professional education existed for military officers to continue to hone their skills as they advanced in rank and responsibility.

In 1901, the War Department created the military education system.[46] Regular Army officers demonstrating the potential for increased responsibility advanced to schooling. Some new schools included infantry, cavalry, artillery, engineering, and medical schools.[47] The best officers went to the Army War College at the height of their careers.

---

45 Doubler, p. 78
46 Doubler, p. 123
47 Ibid.

They engaged in advanced studies, current military policy matters, and plans for War Department consideration.

Due to the nature of the citizen-soldier, it was always tricky for National Guard soldiers to participate in the Army school system. A National Guard soldier must leave his business, farm, or employment to attend military training. Most Guard officers could not afford to take a year away from their jobs to participate in full-time schooling, and those who did complained of prejudice against the citizen-soldiers among the instructors.[48]

Today, due to the nature of the Guard and their civilian lives, some of the required professional military education can be done at home via distance learning, or the courses are shortened.

Logan wrote about the American citizen-soldiers because of his ability to rise above the economic class he was born into, which led to his direct interest in government. Like other militia/National Guard advocates, Logan also served in Congress.

Meanwhile, Logan's contemporary, Major General Upton, was one of the most influential reformers of the Regular Army.

Major General Emory Upton

According to Major General Upton (1839-1881), distrust of the citizen-soldier had a lasting embedded legacy in the Regular Army. After the Spanish-American War, Emory Upton saw no use for the militia. He considered militia officers to be amateurs.

Major General Emory Upton was a Civil War hero and a strong proponent for Regular Army policy reforms. In his book, *Military Policy of the United States,* he argued "that all the defects of the American military system rested upon a fundamental, underlying flaw, excessive civilian control of the military."[49] He believed in the total independence of the Army from civilian control.

---

48 Doubler, p. 133
49 Cassidy, R. "Prophets or Praetorians? The Uptonian Paradox and the Powell Corollary." *The US Army War College Quarterly,* Vol. 33, No. 3, https://press.armywarcollege.edu/cgi/viewcontent.cgi?article=2158&context=parameters.

He openly questioned the value of the Guard and wanted to increase the size of the Regular forces and federal Reserve. One benefit of a federal reserve would be that states could not intervene with the deployment of the part-time force. He argued that American dependence on the citizen-soldier had to be eliminated, along with the reliance on civilian-military control.[50]

Upton recommended a professional military school, a general staff, military evaluations, and promotions based on merit. In Upton's unpublished manuscript, found after his death, he detailed the citizen-soldiers' poor performance and amateurism. Inspired by the Prussian military system, he was the first to advocate for a European-style federal reserve system to augment the Regular Army as needed.[51]

Upton's distaste for the militia and its ties to partisan politics was embedded in the collective culture of the Regular Army officer corp. The professional officers who adopted Upton's views of the citizen-soldier became known as "Uptonians." These men were a powerful influence on military policy over the next century.

Uptonians believed the Guard lacked discipline and professional military skills. They believed the National Guard officers could lead their units in peacetime, but they were not effective enough to lead in battle.[52]

Starting in 1880, Regular Army officers were assigned to assist and inspect National Guard training.

John McAuley Palmer

John McAuley Palmer (1870-1955) was a professional active-duty officer who graduated from the US Military Academy and the Army War College. He served as an advisor on military policy to the War Department General Staff throughout WWII and retired with the rank of Brigadier General.

Throughout his life, he advocated for universal military service and the role of the citizen-soldier. Palmer argued that traditional military

---

50 Doubler, pp. 110, 117, 127
51 Ibid.
52 Ibid.

policy was to have a small Regular Army in peacetime, which could be expanded by mobilizing the mass of citizenry into an Army led by citizen-soldiers.[53]

He influenced our compromise of instituting a military force that included the Regular Army, Reserves, and the National Guard. Our current force is primarily based on his ideas. In 1912, Secretary of War Stimson was so impressed with Palmer's writings that he included them in his annual report. The plan included full integration of the National Guard.

Palmer wrote, "It is the traditional policy of the United States that the military establishment in the time of peace is to be a small Regular Army and that the ultimate war force of the Nation is to be a great army of citizen-soldiers. This fundamental theory of military organization is sound economically and politically."[54]

He was a lone voice against Major General Emory Upton.

National Guard Association

In 1878, the National Guard Association (NGA) was formed. Today, the organization is the National Guard Association of the United States (NGAUS). The purpose of this citizen-soldier lobbying group was to advocate for National Guard policies at the federal level. The early founders of the NGA believed that because the National Guard represented mostly citizens, they could lobby Congress. The early leaders wanted militia reform and funding.

The NGA is the nation's oldest and most successful military lobbying organization.[55] In 1903, the NGA persuaded Congress to increase the Guard's annual appropriation from $400,000 to $1 million.

Charles Dick

Further links between politics and military policy were established by Charles W.F. Dick (1858-1945). He was Commander of the Ohio

---

53 "History of U.S. Military Policy." *RAND Corporation,* https://www.rand.org/pubs/tools/TL238/tool.html.

54 McAuley, John. "Palmer and the Reserve Components." *US Army War College Quarterly: Parameters* Volume 12, Number 1.

55 Doubler, p. 104

Division National Guard and a US Senator. In 1902, he was elected as NGA president and held the position for seven years. While in Congress, he championed the 1903 and 1908 Dick Acts.[56]

The 1903 Dick Act provided that National Guard soldiers would be paid for summer camp – but not the monthly drills. In 1910, the NGA lobbied Congress for drill pay. The War Department pushed back on this point and demanded more control over the Guard. National Guard leaders and the War Department were at loggerheads over the issue for about six years.[57] As part of the National Defense Act of 1916, Guard leaders secured drill pay in exchange for permitting more stringent controls and oversight by the Regular Army.

Guard advocates could see the momentum building against using the National Guard.

Early Cost-Benefit Analysis

An early member of the NGA pointed out that the Regular Army of 26,000 officers and men cost the taxpayers $40 million yearly, while the militia allotment was $200,000 yearly.[58] The investment in the militia was the best return on the taxpayer's dollars.

Another observer calculated that the annual cost of maintaining one Regular was $1,000, while a Guardsman only cost $24. He pointed out that the states and citizen-soldiers took on 80% of the financial burden.[59] The cost-benefit of the Guard has been a recurring argument regarding their advantage.

Challenges at the Border Crisis

President Wilson called the Guard for a crisis at the southern border with mixed results in 1916. The Guard responded and deployed their forces from all over the country. In terms of logistics, the distance Guardsmen could rapidly travel with their horses was impressive. However, many of the Guard soldiers needed to be more fit, and many needed to improve physical standards.

56 Ibid., p. 146
57 Ibid., p. 131
58 Ibid., p. 105
59 Ibid., p. 111

When the Guard arrived for their mission, the War Department was unprepared to receive them. The Guardsmen endured poor facilities with intense heat. Their moods soured as they were regulated to security duty rather than combat.[60]

Major Douglas MacArthur said, "When one considers the number of men moved and the distance they were moved, the recent mobilization… was the best job of its kind done by any country."[61]

Nevertheless, leaders from the various camps saw that the Guard needed improvements in training, equipment, and manpower.

World War I

Bitterness over officer assignments in National Guard units occurred in both World Wars.

General "Blackjack" Pershing commanded the American Expeditionary Forces in World War I. General Pershing testified in a Congressional hearing after the war, saying, "The National Guard never received the wholehearted support of the Regular Army during the World War. There was always more or less prejudice against them…"[62]

There were a considerable number of Guard combat officers who lost their posts to Regular and Reserve officers. The Guard officers served in staff positions, while the Regular Army served in primary roles. Tensions over relieving Guard officers of their command ran very high, especially within the divisions. The Guard officers must have felt affronted at this doubt of their capabilities. At the same time, Guard soldiers well-accustomed to serving under their Guard commanders were unhappy at the sudden change in the command structure and considered it disrespectful to the officers they admired.

At World War I's end, Upton's belief in the Regular Army was reinvigorated. A call went out to eliminate the Guard and increase the Reserve force. However, the plan had little support in Congress.

---

60 Ibid., p. 143
61 Ibid., p. 143
62 Ibid., p. 165

In 1919, Senator James W. Wadsworth, a former Guardsman from New York and Chairman of the Senate Military Affairs Committee, held hearings on military policy.

General John O'Ryan, New York National Guard Division Commander in WWI, testified in the Wadsworth committee hearings. O'Ryan was the 27th Division Commander from New York. His men admired him so much that they created their division patch with N and Y and a constellation of stars, a visual pun on the constellation Orion. He was the youngest division commander in the American Expeditionary Force and the only member of the Guard to retain his command during the war. O'Ryan's testimony proposed that the Guard have full involvement in the national defense under the Army clause in the Constitution.

Colonel John Palmer, discussed previously, also testified. Palmer impressed Senator Wadsworth so much that the senator had Palmer assigned as an advisor to the Military Affairs Committee and used him to write legislation.

World War II

In the Second World War, Lieutenant General Leslie J. McNair, Commander of the Army Ground Forces, was responsible for all the Army training in the United States. McNair, a Regular Army officer Uptonian, felt hatred toward the National Guard soldiers and believed they contributed little to the national defense. After he visited the 30th Division, an Ohio National Guard unit, as they trained for war, he described the Guard's leadership as "the blind leading the blind."[63] He believed the National Guard generals were unprofessional and unfit for their rank.

However, the 30th Division landed in Normandy ten days after D-Day and had remarkable combat records. Division soldiers received twelve Medals of Honor, more than any other division in the American Expeditionary Forces.[64]

While the Regulars looked down on the Guardsmen, the same was true on the other side—institutional bias among the Guardsmen against the

---

63   Ibid., p. 175
64   Ibid., p. 163

Regulars existed due to their poor treatment as mobilization stations were established. A deep divide between the two components existed.

Influence of the Cold War

After the World Wars, Regular Army forces were reduced to minimal strength. But that changed during the Cold War. The National Security Council (NSC) 68 supported the Regular Army in obtaining more men, money, and equipment. This document set the stage for the struggle between communism and democracy; the only outcome could be victory or defeat. We needed a full-time war machine to deter the Soviet Union in Western Europe, succeed in our arms race, and create a military-industrial complex including defense contractors, research labs, technology, lobby groups, and trillions of dollars.

NSC 68 promoted the need for a large military and defense industry.

Combine Reserve Components

Through the years, there have been several attempts to combine the Reserves and the National Guard.

In 1947, Secretary of Defense (SecDef) James Forestall convened a panel that the DOD called the "Gray Board" to find ways to abolish the National Guard. The board recommended the merger of the two organizations. However, the lobby groups for both the Guard and Reserves successfully lobbied against it.

In 1964, SecDef Robert McNamara recommended the same thing. He aimed to merge both components under the Guard to reduce redundancy. Congress rejected the plan.

1993 SecDef Les Aspen wanted the DOD to do a bottom-up review of the roles and readiness of the military. The National Guard was balanced with a combat force, combat support, and combat service support. The Reserves would align with combat support and combat service support.

Creighton William Abrams, Jr.

Creighton Williams Abrams, Jr. (1914-1975) saw a direct link between the civilian world and military occupations in combat service support in the Reserve components. He knew some Reserve soldiers practiced their wartime mission daily during their civilian careers. General Abram's "Total Force" policy was essential to using the Reserve forces as vital to national security.

With the Vietnam War behind him, General Creighton Abrams, Army Chief of Staff, wanted a force to mix Regular and Reserve forces. The 1970s "Total Force" policy was created to balance political pressures with the desire to maintain active-duty strength. After the war, there was pressure to reduce the Regular Army's size and increase the Reserve size. Abrams created the round out brigades in the National Guard and moved a lot of combat support and combat service support units to the Reserve forces.

To fight a prolonged war outside of the United States, the president would have to call on the Reserve components, and the Reserve forces would have to be resourced at equal levels to the Regular Army. The theory of the round out National Guard brigades was tested in 1990.

Desert Shield and Desert Storm

With the Cold War over, the military budget was under heavy scrutiny. The debate over the proper role and size of the National Guard was once again reenergized. When Saddam Hussein attacked Kuwait on August 2, 1990, the Bush administration focused on committing US ground troops to Saudi Arabia.

King Fahd of Saudi Arabia requested American assistance on August 7, 1990. That day, the Central Command initiated Operation Desert Shield.

The Army divisions deployed rapidly to Saudi Arabia without their National Guard round out brigades. The National Guard brigades remained in the United States, awaiting their mobilization orders.

Central Command needed the Army National Guard and Reserves for the vital logistical system to win the war, but the combat units remained in the rear awaiting orders.

On August 22, President Bush signed Executive Order No. 12727 authorizing the DOD to mobilize Reserves. On August 23, Secretary Cheney said the National Guard was only to provide combat support and combat service support units. He stated there was no authority for combat units.[65] In other words, the National Guard round out brigades would not deploy, completely defying the Abrams policy of the "Total Force" and round out brigade concept.

The Department of Defense stated that the need was immediate and that the National Guard combat brigades would take too long.

House Armed Service Committee members wrote letters criticizing Secretary of Defense Cheney and the Department of Defense's failure to send the National Guard round out brigades.

When President Bush decided to increase the size of the force on the ground, he issued Executive Order 12733, which authorized the use of combat units. However, combat units and round out brigades were never deployed to the Middle East.

At a press conference, Secretary Cheney and General Colin L. Powell, chairman of the Joint Chiefs of Staff (JCS), said the National Guard units would have to undergo extensive training, including a rotation at the National Training Center, to ensure they were combat-ready.[66]

One of the round out brigades was the 48th Infantry Brigade from Georgia. While most of the unit was preparing to train at Fort Irwin, California, the staff officers attended an eight-day course at Fort Leavenworth, Kansas. The time spent together resulted in friction between the brigade's leadership and the Regular Army.[67] The active-duty leadership insisted that the Guard unit abandon its standard procedures and adopt unfamiliar practices. The situation created confusion and broke down the staff cohesion.

---

65   Doubler, p. 263
66   Ibid., p. 269
67   Ibid., p. 270

While the brigade never deployed to the Middle East, the 48th did remarkably well at the National Training Center at Fort Irwin, California. The Guard Brigade headquarters was the first Army headquarters to maneuver three combined-arms Task Forces in the open desert.

The Army's non-use of a National Guard maneuver brigade had people speculating on both sides. Either they were concerned that the Guard would fail and put the Task Force's mission in jeopardy or that they would succeed and threaten the existence of the active-duty divisions.[68]

Some even argued that the 48th Brigade was more expeditionary and ready than the active-duty forces because of all the training they had completed at the National Training Center at Fort Irwin, California.

A Seat at the Table

In the 1990s, the struggle over resources and the reduction in military size created new tensions. Army proponents believed the National Guard could not be trained in less than a year, implying they were obsolete, despite evidence against the contrary, such as the Guard's involvement and accomplishments during previous wars.[69] During this time, active-duty leadership often kept the Guard's leadership away from crucial decisions.

Real change began after 9/11, Hurricane Katrina, and other incidents in which the National Guard proved its worth.

On November 10, 2011, the Senate Arms Service Committee held a hearing regarding putting the Chief of the National Guard (CNG) on the Joint Chiefs of Staff. The head of the Joint Chiefs told hearing members that "putting the CNG at the table would not solve any problems. The Guard is already represented by the active-duty members at the table."

Senator Lindsay Graham was a champion for the National Guard. At the hearing, he said, "The institution resisted Goldwater-Nicolas; the institution resisted having the Commandant of the Marine Corps on

---

68 Ibid., p. 285
69 Ibid., p. 312

the JCS. I think we should consider the time has come, given the post-September 11 duties of the National Guard, to have a seat at the table. It doesn't change command authority, doesn't turn the work upside down."[70] Despite the fervent objection by all the active-duty service chiefs, the change was part of the 2012 NDAA. The National Guard had a seat at the table.

Top-Down versus Bottom-Up Tensions

Troops on the ground, the ones who carry the weapons, follow the orders, do the work, and take most of the risks, are naturally competitive and proud of their military. High-level tensions created by the government and bureaucracy, as those officials compete for resources, may trickle down somewhat into the attitudes of officers and soldiers.

In the years following the Vietnam War, significant personal tensions existed between branches because the National Guard was never sent to participate.

However, my knowledge of the past few decades and personal experience can attest that the "tensions" between military groups are generally good-natured, no different than any rivalry that may emerge when two or more groups are brought together to serve a purpose. Soldiers are not foolish enough to let branch rivalries interfere with their duties.

Ordinarily, at the ground level, the Regular Army, Army Reservists, and Army National Guard work together very well and without animosity, with what amounts to friendly competition at most, and certainly without interfering with their duties. The training of the National Guard has become so sophisticated that their presence is always a welcome addition.

Summary

In summarizing this chapter, I'd like to share a quote from John A. Logan, who wrote, "But no record of the war would be wholly just that failed to portray the unique character of the American citizen-soldier, and no deduction from the lessons of the conflict can cover the

---

70   US Senate 2011 testimony

ultimate logic of the case that does not consider as one of the premises this character of the soldier as it bears upon the future of his country."[71]

The modern Guard has gone through quite a journey to become the force it is today. In its early forms, the constitutional militias were a decentralized force that required each governor to train and administer their citizen-soldiers. The militias needed more standardization in training, uniforms, equipment, and administration. The military skills of the militia men varied from each state. The resources in each state also varied, and some needed more for a militia.

Through no fault of the citizen-soldier or the governors, the idealism in the founding document created an unrealistic military structure for a future world power.

The United States federal government needed more control of the military's actions. A Regular Army, composed of professional officers, replaced the militia's position as the primary national defense method. Yet, the transition to the Regular Army sparked deep criticism of the militia/National Guard, especially when resources were tight.

The National Guard has a noticeable financial advantage. Considering all the operational, maintenance, and personnel expenses, the National Guard costs about 31% of the active component.[72] The National Guard also brings together the market economy with the government, providing skilled soldiers with little cost to the government. For example, the federal government military receives the skills of farmers, teachers, nurses, network engineers, etc., without the cost of training.

Generally speaking, the "tensions" between military groups happen at the bureaucratic level. Among the decision-makers, fighting for a military's relevance is a resource battle. At the ground level, soldiers do their duty with respect and camaraderie for each other.

---

71 Logan, J.A, (n.d) *The soldier of America*. Google Books. https://books.google.com/books/about/The_Volunteer_Soldier_of_America.html?id=-XYPAAAAYAAJ.
72 The White Paper in the tablet file 17 FEB 12

CHAPTER 6

History of the Militia and Civil Unrest

Civil unrest created our country. Civil unrest drove English citizens to seek a new life across the ocean, and it later compelled them to fight for freedom from tyranny.

Civil unrest in the American colonies began with Samuel Adams and the patriots in Boston. The Boston Tea Party was a violent action by a patriotic mob against the British Parliament.[73] Protesting British rule was a keystone of America's foundation and figured heavily in the evolution of the militia.

As discussed in previous chapters, the Posse Comitatus Act (18 USC 1385) primarily prohibits using federal forces to enforce state and federal laws. However, active forces may provide indirect support, such as logistics and training, when the Secretary of Defense approves. Congress passed exceptions to the Posse Comitatus Act so federal forces can act temporarily and urgently when lives or property are in danger.

The Posse Comitatus Act laid the foundation for governors to use their National Guard to establish peace and stability within their states. Yet the federal government largely funds the National Guard, so its troops train for war on a Title 32 status. This federally funded training ensures the Guard's seamless integration into active duty during times of war.

The Guard is measured against their federal counterparts, even though the Guard only consumes a fraction of the training time and funding of the Regular Army on duty 24/7. The fact that the part-time, citizen-

---

73   Doubler, p. 35

based force has been largely successful in both combat and domestic operations is an impressive tribute to this unique American fighting force.

Most of the time, the Guard supports local law enforcement without issues. However, there have been times when things went awry. This chapter looks at notable instances of the early militias' and National Guard's performances during the early tax rebellions in the United States, the evolution of the Posse Comitatus, and the rare occasions when things went wrong.

When does a protest become a civil disturbance?[74]

In most of the instances I reference in this chapter and the next, the actions of civilians begin as protests against government actions or decisions. The Constitution's First Amendment gives United States citizens the right to assemble and express views; protests and demonstrations are legal. Hundreds of protests occur annually nationwide without any significant problems.

Protesters must follow specific laws when demonstrating in public forums (private forums have somewhat different standards), including observation of safety and traffic laws. Protestors cannot assemble so that public safety is endangered (for instance, they cannot block entrances to buildings, emergency exits, or block the flow of street traffic without obtaining a parade permit or other permission from the local authorities). Counter-protesters can also be present and within sight and hearing of the protesting group.

Some form of law enforcement is almost always present at such gatherings to ensure everyone remains safe and that public operations continue without interruption. If the protest matter is controversial, officials may call out greater law enforcement numbers. Law enforcement reminds everyone—protestors, counter-protestors, and bystanders alike—to behave orderly.

Police officers may separate antagonistic groups if they believe violence could break out, but the groups can remain within sight and hearing distance. Other laws that protection agencies must follow include

74   Information in this section provided by the American Civil Liberties Union at aclu.org.

treating protesters and counter-protesters equally. Most of the time, the participants behave orderly; likewise, protective agencies perform their duties well.

By their nature, public protests are usually scenes of significant dispute, and emotions may run high. People don't go to the trouble of attending protests (or raising forces, in the case of earlier American rebellions) if they don't care about their cause and believe they are on the right side. We all know how hard it can be to control emotional outrage; this certainly becomes harder in crowds surrounded by others as angry as we are. The concept of mob mentality works on us: we have an innate desire to fit in with those around us. Unfortunately, that desire affects our decision-making logic.

On the same lines, law enforcement bodies ostensibly must remain impartial. Still, they, too, are human, and in such stressful circumstances, mistakes and misunderstandings can occur and quickly spiral out of control. Actions or words can be misinterpreted. It doesn't take much to cause panic amidst large groups of anxious people.

Mob mentality affects everyone, not just protesters.

A protest (or any public gathering of any size) becomes a civil disturbance if it disrupts a community and requires intervention to maintain public safety. Should that happen, the question often is *who started* the trouble. Was it the protesters, the counter-protesters, the law enforcement, or other outside circumstances? That is often the subject of an extensive investigation if a civil disturbance results in damages, injuries, or even deaths. Sometimes, the answer is never straightforward.

Therefore, over the next two chapters, we'll reflect on times when militia groups were part of rebellions or disturbances where violence broke out. As we examine riots, looting, and other criminal or dangerous behaviors, up to and including actual insurrection, we should remember that anger combined with mob mentality is a serious catalyst for violence, that it can happen to almost anyone, and that "protesting" itself is not the problem. Our freedom to express dissatisfaction with the status quo leads to progress, compromise, and social change.

Early American Rebellions

The first thing that caused sufficient anger to raise militias and require militia response was taxation, which is no surprise. The newly formed United States attributed a significant part of its decision to split from Great Britain to widespread anger and discontent over taxation without representation. While the young country felt its way through infancy, citizens often reacted poorly to the unpleasantly familiar feeling of taxes levied on their livelihoods and property. The following incidents, now termed "rebellions," are those instances of protest that resulted in the movement of entire armies against one another, as laws were broken and lives endangered.

Shays' Rebellion

The Articles of Confederation faced a domestic insurrection just three years after the Revolutionary War. Daniel Shays was a disgruntled veteran of Bunker Hill and a former Continental Army officer. He saw that veterans received little pay from the war but were responsible for tax debts.

In September 1786, Shays led an insurrection against the State of Massachusetts because of the debts, taxes, and the threat of land seizures. The protestors started small, interrupting tax collection and repossessions, but as their numbers grew, they eventually shut down several state courts. Their actions had a dual purpose: to cause inconvenience and express their discontent with the judicial process.

Neither the state nor the weak federal government could raise funds to put down the rebellion, which instilled fear in the other states' political leadership. The problem was compounded because many local militiamen, who ostensibly protected local courts, sided with the insurgents. A volunteer militia from eastern Massachusetts finally ended the spreading rebellion in 1787.

Shays' Rebellion, as it came to be known, convinced the states and Congress that a stronger, more organized central government was needed to deal with domestic unrest. Some scholars believe this rebellion played a significant role in creating, formatting, and ratifying the United States Constitution, as it marked apparent deficiencies in the Articles of Confederation.

Whiskey Rebellion

Less than a decade later, in 1791, a tax on distilled spirits was passed, by which the government intended to raise funds to pay Revolutionary War debts. No other domestic product had been taxed thus far. American farmers, many of whom were Revolutionary War veterans who used their surplus grains to distill whiskey, resisted this tax. Whiskey had become such an essential commodity that it was often a medium of exchange. Why should they pay these federal taxes after fighting a war that supposedly opposed taxation without local representation? Protestors intimidated national tax collectors, and local enforcement was difficult to achieve because so many of the militia were against the whiskey tax themselves. The rebellion simmered and grew over the following three years.

President Washington believed the revolt was direct resistance against the central government's authority. He used the Calling Forth Act of 1792 to respond to the rebellion. However, some states had difficulty filling their quota because of opposition to the tax. Nevertheless, Washington rode with almost 13,000 militia, a relatively intimidating number at the time, provided from Virginia, Maryland, New Jersey, and Pennsylvania.

The militia's notable size served as a deterrent, which may have been its real purpose. The rebels went home before the overwhelming force arrived. There was no confrontation. The event displayed a coordinated effort as many states organized to put down an insurrection successfully. The militia reinforced the legitimacy of the new government.[75]

Fries' Rebellion of 1799

This rebellion in Pennsylvania from 1799-1800 was an armed conflict led by John Fries against the taxation imposed on real estate and enslaved people. The government attempted to raise funds for a potential war against France through this tax. The popularity of the resistance increased throughout the state, mainly due to rabble-rousing

75   Doubler, p. 72

and rumors that fired up the German immigrant population. The local militia and other armed men harassed and intimidated the tax collectors, who had the unenviable task of traveling town-to-town and assessing properties in front of their owners, which was seen as a suspicious invasion of privacy.

The authorities arrested some rebels, but the men escaped with the help of nearly 400 other rebels who marched on the prison in Bethlehem, Pennsylvania, to free them. President John Adams controlled the situation with federal troops and local militia arresting the insurgents.[76]

The Insurrection Act of 1807

President Thomas Jefferson signed the Insurrection Act in 1807 to prevent his former Vice President Aaron Burr from raising an army and taking territory in Mexico.

Even though he was never charged with murder, Burr's political career was ruined after he killed Alexander Hamilton in a duel. Burr had nothing to lose and believed he might form an empire by gathering and arming his force, then taking territory in Louisiana and Mexico.[77] At the time, Jefferson had no constitutional authority to stop Burr's army with federal forces. He worked with Congress to get a new law on the books.

After Congress passed the Insurrection Act, Burr had already been in custody for eleven days.[78]

The Insurrection Act provided the exception to Posse Comitatus, though the Posse Comitatus Act would only become law after Reconstruction. The Insurrection Act allows the president to use active-duty forces and federalize the National Guard to suppress insurrection and rebellions.

It's interesting to note that the basis for the Insurrection Act originated with a former vice president and his motivation for power.

76 Wikipedia contributors. "Fries's Rebellion." *Wikipedia, The Free Encyclopedia*, 2023, https://en.wikipedia.org/wiki/Fries%27s_Rebellion

77 "The Burr Conspiracy." *American Experience*, PBS, https://www.pbs.org/wgbh/americanexperience/features/duel-burr-conspiracy/.

78 Roos, Dave. "Thomas Jefferson Signed the Insurrection Act in 1807 to Foil a Plot by Aaron Burr." *History*, A&E Television Networks, 2020, https://www.history.com/news/insurrection-act-thomas-jefferson-aaron-burr.

The law has been used to undermine American Indian territories. President Lincoln used this law in 1861 to send federal troops into the South during the Civil War and Reconstruction. Otherwise, it has been chiefly used to send in federal troops to break up labor disputes and stabilize racial protests.

Violence in Westward Expansion

Protecting against Native American attacks, as well as performing counterattacks, was a significant militia function. As pioneers moved into unregulated and largely unprotected lands, they faced numerous dangers, including attacks by indigenous tribes. Forming a militia was the only available option for the organized protection of these small, distant communities.

As we know in hindsight, such battles were more than "protests" and could hardly be classified as "civil disturbances." The actions were brutal, the pretense of protection tainted by misunderstanding and hatred. I include this topic as another example of when the militia overreacted or committed questionable acts. Their reasoning may have seemed justified then, but looking back, we can see when terrible injustice was done.

A Sioux uprising in 1862 killed 600 people. The Minnesota militia eventually put down the rebellion. In Colorado in 1864, militiamen killed and mutilated nearly 150 Native Americans while most of the tribe's men were away hunting. The militia went to Denver and displayed 100 human scalps they had collected from their victims.[79] These were just two of many shocking incidences of violence between the militia and Native Americans.

Active-duty forces took on the responsibility of fighting Native Americans after the 1860s. The Wounded Knee Massacre in 1890 killed around 200 Lakota Indians, marking the climax of the US Army's effort to repress indigenous American tribes on the plains.

Labor Disputes

The Great Railroad Strike of 1877, in which workers protesting poor wages stopped railroad operations, saw the rise of militia for domestic

---

79   Ibid, p. 106

operations. Fifteen states called out approximately 45,000 militiamen to support local authorities in clashes between labor unions and the railroads.

In some cases, the militia fired on strikers; in others, they united with the workers.[80] The failure of the militia to control the strikes led to federal forces being used in several states. These multi-state strikes saw at least 100 people killed and far more injured.

The increased use of the militia for labor disputes identified the National Guard as the protector of big industry. The situation worsened when industrial leaders provided private funding for their protection.[81] In time, the Guard became known as a protector of the "robber barons." This was a label that Guard advocates wanted to eliminate as quickly as possible.

Summary

Until the turn of the 19th Century, militia and the National Guard were typically used to quell outright rebellions that had gathered armed forces, protect those otherwise vulnerable to the new territories they explored, or step in to regulate labor disputes. We have noted several instances where the militia's actions were questionable, either due to the motivations of the controlling powers (such as the president or large corporations) or because there was little or no regulation on their actions (which could occur in Westward expansion).

Following the Railroad Strike of 1877, Guard advocates wanted to shake the robber baron stereotype in exchange for combat missions in major conflicts. The Guard advocates were successful; we've already discussed the National Guard's extensive history in combat during World Wars I and II and the Korean War.

The Posse Comitatus Act of 1878 prohibited the Army from supporting civil authorities unless the president ordered it, ensuring that governors would continue to rely on the National Guard for law enforcement.

---

80   Ibid., p. 102
81   Ibid., p. 103

This act remains legislation governing the use of Regular and National Guard forces for domestic operations.[82]

The face of civil disturbances changed dramatically in the second half of the 20th Century and beyond. Let's examine how the Civil Rights movement, the Vietnam War, and milestone incidences since that time have affected perceptions of protests, protesters, and the National Guard.

---

82   Ibid., p. 104

CHAPTER 7

The Forces of Change

The 1960s were extraordinarily turbulent in the United States.

The civil rights movement, which campaigned to end laws supporting racial segregation, disenfranchisement, and discrimination, was active before and throughout the decade.

Morale in the country dropped when Lee Harvey Oswald shot President John F. Kennedy on November 22, 1963.

The United States sent the first combat troops to Vietnam in March 1965.

In July of the same year, President Johnson increased the draft for US military forces from 17,000 to 35,000. Citizens came out in droves to protest both the war and the draft.

Martin Luther King, Jr. was assassinated on April 4, 1968, and Robert F. Kennedy was assassinated only two months later.

The decade was marked by a dramatically changing culture, a time of immense bravery, creativity, violence, and confusion. It was an age of new paradigms and freedom but also new cynicism and fear. The change came with considerable stressors and growing pains. Civil unrest flared repeatedly across the nation.

Particularly with so many forces deployed to Vietnam, the National Guard was the only organization with the equipment, workforce, and logistical capability to assist local law enforcement with civil unrest.

Civil Rights Protests and Riots

Watts Riots

The Watts Riots (August 11-16, 1965) started after a confrontation between the California Highway Patrol and African American Marquette Frye, his brother Ronald, and his mother Rena Price. Frye resisted arrest for drunk driving and was struck in the face with a baton in front of a gathering crowd, and tempers flared. Allegations of police brutality spread quickly through Watts and surrounding neighborhoods. The situation, involving looting and firebombing, escalated until elected officials had to call on the Guard to support law enforcement. The Guard created roadblocks, confronted angry crowds, and protected firefighters as blazes were put out.

The National Guard and police made heavy use of firearms. Reports of sniper fire increased. Many were injured by mistake.[83] The riot resulted in 34 deaths, 4,000 arrests, and $35 million in property damages. The riot shocked the United States and uncovered the realities of racial tensions.[84] By the time the riots ended, more than 13,000 Guardsmen were on duty there.

Summer of 1967

Not quite two years later, the US saw mass rioting in over 100 cities. Most riots were sparked after an altercation between White police officers and Black citizens. The worst rioting happened during two weeks in July in Newark and Detroit.[85]

Fear spread throughout Detroit; the citizens, police, and National Guard were all frightened.[86] The governor wanted to bring in federal forces. President Johnson signed a proclamation federalizing the Michigan National Guard and authorizing the use of paratroopers. About 5,000 National Guardsmen were in the city, but they lacked adequate training and suffered profound fatigue; many guardsmen traveled 200 miles

---

83 Anonymous. "Kerner Commission Report on the Causes, Events, and Aftermaths of the Civil Disorders of 1967." National Advisory Commission on Civil Disorders, Report p. 37, 1967.

84 Ibid.

85 Ibid., p. 15

86 Ibid., p. 20

and then worked 30 hours without rest.[87] Most received on-the-spot mob control and riot-control training but were outfitted with machine guns and tanks. The combination of exhaustion, incomplete training, and dangerous weaponry proved catastrophic.

There were accidental shootings. A tank sprayed a building with .50-caliber tracer bullets, only to find out later that the building was empty.

The general mass confusion caused many deaths of innocent bystanders. The police and National Guard were involved in numerous shootouts; in some cases, gunfire between law enforcement and protestors lasted several hours.

Other matters seemed simply unprofessional. A Guardsman who was riding in a firetruck accidentally discharged his weapon and blew a hole through a roof after the truck hit a bump.[88] The Guard received heavy criticism and unfavorable comparisons to the active-duty paratroopers, who were able to bring more peace and stability to Detroit.

A week later, President Johnson ordered the Pentagon to establish procedures for the Guard to train and receive equipment for future protests and riots.

Tampa Riot 1967

The National Guard supplemented the local police after several days of protesting and rioting following the fatal shooting of a 19-year-old Black man named Martin Chambers.[89] Most of the rioting occurred on June 11, within the 12 hours following Mr. Chamber's lethal shooting; a crowd of some 500 people formed the initial protest, their anger spreading throughout the city as the police presence initially withdrew. Response was slow, and severe damage was done to Tampa districts.

---

87 "A Time of Tragedy." The Detroit News, August 11, 1967,. https:lsa.umich.edu/sid/detroiters-speak/detroiters-speak-archive/_jcr_content/par/download_1667472917/file.res/"A%20Time%20of%20Tragedy"%20Article%20from%20the%20Detroit%20News.

88 Ibid.

89 Kerner Report, p. 42

When the National Guard arrived the following day, they supported police forces in creating perimeters around the unstable areas of town. An estimated 475 National Guardsmen patrolled around an area called the Central Park Village, where most of the rioting took place.

Large African American populations complained about the National Guard's presence in these areas. The community leaders replaced some of the Guard with young individuals who needed work, so the "White Hats" Youth Patrol was adopted, supported by the Hillsborough County Sheriff's Department, to maintain order within these perimeters. The group disbanded not long after the riots occurred for unrelated reasons.

Newark Riot 1967

The Mayor of Newark requested National Guard support along with the state police after burning, looting, rioting, and the siege of a police station. About 100 National Guardsmen supported the police after a startling incident with an African American escalated tension throughout the city.

While on duty, a Guardsman fired a shot to scare a man away, as the Guardsmen had been ordered to keep people away from a building. However, the situation was already tense. Confusion overtook the police and National Guardsmen present, who believed they were under sniper fire.[90]

The Guard set up over 100 roadblocks while the state police and riot teams prepared to regain city control. Reports of snipers were rampant. Major General James F. Cantwell, Chief of Staff of the New Jersey National Guard, testified before the Armed Service Subcommittee of House Representatives that "there was too much firing initially against snipers."

The Director of Police told the Commission that the situation was so bad, "Guardsmen were firing upon police, and police were firing back at them." In this situation, the National Guard lacked riot training. They were described as "young and scared."

---

90   Ibid., p. 19

Active-duty soldiers attempted to bring normalcy to the situation. However, the National Guard continued with loaded weapons, shooting out the streetlights. The Guard ordered people off the street and into their homes and shot one person for failing to respond.[91] Pictures of the area look like a combat zone from a third-world nation. Forty-three people were killed in the riots, including one National Guardsman. The National Guard killed at least seven of those people.

Kerner Report, 1967

President Lyndon Johnson established the National Advisory Commission on Violence and Civil Disorders, otherwise known as the Kerner Commission. Its task was to determine the cause of racial unrest in American cities.

The report found the need for better training and riot gear for the National Guard to aid in civil disturbance control. The Kerner Report also noted that because the National Guard primarily consisted of White men, confronting Black rioters caused tension and called for increased Black participation in the Guard.[92] While important, the results of the Kerner Report were not timely enough to respond to the most devastating civil rights protests of 1968.

The Assassination of Martin Luther King, Jr.

The worst riots of the 1960s exploded in April 1968, when Martin Luther King, Jr.'s assassination catalyzed the eruption of grief and outrage.[93] King's campaign for civil rights promoted peaceful change; his death was heartbreaking to those who had heard his fierce and dignified message of equity. The Guard kept the peace in Detroit, Washington, Chicago, and Baltimore as furious crowds of protestors and counter-protestors surged.[94]

---

91   Ibid., p. 73
92   Ibid, p. 228
93   Ibid, p. 226
94   Ibid, p. 228

Government Protests and Riots

Kent State

Kent State is most infamously remembered of all the civil disturbances during the Vietnam era because while it started as a peace protest, its nature transformed as protestors objected to the presence of the Guard. While the first two days of the protests were because of the invasion of Cambodia, the last two days were in response to Guardsmen on Campus.

On April 30, 1970, President Nixon ordered an invasion of Cambodia. This action prompted widespread antiwar protests across the nation. There was no declaration of war or any appropriate act by Congress. Strikes and protests erupted in approximately 400 different schools. After Nixon announced, violent antiwar protests reached college campuses in Kent, Ohio.

On May 1, students gathered around Kent bars. The crowd hazed police officers, and some threw bottles at passing patrol cars. The group grew to about 500 students. Some protestors broke windows, and some display items were stolen.

At 12:30 a.m., Mayor LeRoy M. Satrom declared a state of emergency and ordered the bars closed. The mayor banned the sale of alcohol and firearms. Gas could only be sold if it was pumped into a car. His city curfew was set from 8:00 p.m. to 6:00 a.m., but this did not include the university. Kent police pushed the students back to the campus with tear gas. The police would not enter the university campus, however. The crowd dispersed after returning to campus, but city leadership was concerned about lacking the workforce to control a similar situation in the future.

Mayor Satrom requested National Guard support. At this time, Ohio National Guardsmen were already federalized and providing peace during a union strike in Cleveland-Akron. Therefore, transitioning to Kent was easy. During a coordination meeting with the mayor, the Ohio National Guard liaison told university officials that they would not distinguish between the city and the campus if the National Guard was called to protect the city. The Guard could take complete control of the situation.[95] Nevertheless, university leadership wanted to avoid the National Guard on the campus.

The next day, students rallied to protest the university's attitude toward Cambodia, other student demands, and their desire to abolish the ROTC building, which they felt represented the university's support for the war. The ROTC building was engulfed in flames when the Ohio Guardsmen showed up.

At the university, 1,400 Guardsmen supported local law enforcement. Soldiers carried shotguns, M-1 rifles with fixed bayonets, and tear gas launchers.[96] The anti-war protest turned into an anti-Guard protest, as the students resented the Guard and their violent weaponry on campus.

The Guard didn't have permission to go on the university campus. However, General Canterbury, the Ohio Adjutant General and officer in charge on the scene, later said no specific permission was needed because the university was on state property.[97]

At this point, many people were uncertain about the rules and legality of rallies and demonstrations. The governor had used those words, but there existed no official record that a state of emergency was ever sought or obtained.

A Guard officer stated that he was under the impression that the state of emergency permitted "no gatherings or rallies at all."[98] The mayor had placed the city under a state of civil emergency but never banned peaceful rallies. [99]

Governor Rhodes held a press conference on campus. He called the situation "probably the most vicious form of campus-oriented violence yet perpetrated by dissident groups and their allies in the state of Ohio." He said, "We are going to employ every force of law under our authority."[100]

95 The report of the President's Commission on Campus Unrest, https://www.google. com/books/edition/The_Report_of_the_President_s_Commission/KgmcRGYLTYo C?hl=en&gbpv=1&dq=Scranton+Commission+Report,+p.+3&printsec=frontcover&bshm=rimc/1.
96 Ibid., p. 230
97 Ibid., p. 30
98 Ibid., p. 38
99 Ibid., p. 38
100 Ibid., p. 31

Leaflets were distributed that stated the governor, through the National Guard, had assumed control of the campus and that no gatherings were permitted. The Guard was empowered to arrest violators.

As time passed, the peaceful crowd became irritated. People began cursing law enforcement; they started throwing rocks. A military helicopter was used to spotlight students as they moved and ran. Students were ordered to disperse while the Guardsmen put on their gas masks and began moving the crowd.

By this time, the Guard and the police were tired and irritated with the students' behavior. Some Guard had only received three hours of sleep the night before. The soldiers were relieved of duty but required to report back to the streets only a few hours later.

On May 4, 1970, the crowd grew to about 500. General Canterbury ordered the group to disperse. Assembled soldiers locked and loaded their weapons, but the crowd refused to move. The Guard formed shoulder-to-shoulder and was ordered to march across the university common area to disperse the students.

The crowd grew to about 800 people, with another 1,000 in the hills around the common area. The Guard fired tear gas at the crowds, and the students scattered. Guardsmen with gas masks began to move on the group, which united the people against them.

The anger and anxiety between the students and Guard catalyzed catastrophe. Armed with WWII vintage rifles, members of the Ohio National Guard fired at least 61 shots at the crowd. They killed four and wounded nine.[101] Two more students were bayoneted.

The FBI and Counterintelligence Program were the lead agencies in managing Kent State. There was a heated controversy over the shooting. Some argued there was an order to fire on the students. The Ohio National Guard claimed they were under sniper attack.[102]

---

101 The President's Commission on Campus Unrest. "Special Report: The Kent State Tragedy." Scranton Commission, 1970, p. 1, https://omeka.library.kent.edu/special-collections/items/show/3419.

102 Krause, Laurel. "Kent State: Was It about Civil Rights or Murdering Student Protesters?" *Censored 2013: Dispatches from the Media Revolution.* 2012, https://patch.com/ohio/kent/bp--kent-state-was-it-about-civil-rights-or-murdering05547020bf.

The Congressional investigation asked General Canterbury what authority he had to break up the crowd. He replied that the Guard was still mobilized for a Teamsters strike, and the proclamation incorporated the Ohio Riot Act. However, the proclamation did not explicitly mention the Riot Act. Canterbury later told a commission investigator that the Ohio Riot Act permits an officer to order the dispersal of a crowd when it is engaged in activities that pose and create a present danger to the safety of persons or property.

The Ohio Guard Riot Act pre-employment brief on the rule of force was likely familiar to the Ohio Guardsmen; several had participated in at least 22 other civil disturbances. The rules of force include the authorization and use of rifle butts, bayonets, chemicals, and other weapons.[103] The Guardsmen were armed with M-1 rifles, a high-velocity gun with a range of almost two miles. At the time, the Guardsmen wore gas masks that reduced their ability to hear and see. There is no evidence that an order to fire was given.

The grand jury found that the Ohio National Guard was on the scene only to assist civil authority. Martial law was never declared.[104] The court found that the Guard feared severe bodily injury.

People still ask why the "Guard rules" prevented the demonstrations.

Kent State became the model of military suppression of civil disorder that the historical principle of due process forbids.

1973 Wounded Knee

A dissident Native American group forcibly took control of the village of Wounded Knee on Pine Ridge Reservation, South Dakota, in February 1973, choosing the location as a symbolic reference to the Wounded Knee massacre of 1890.

The group held hostages and refused to allow federal agencies in the area for 17 days. The Native Americans' demands ranged from anger over tribal corruption to control of their tribal lands and mineral rights to the school curriculum.[105]

---

103 Ibid., page 81
104 Ibid., page 4
105 Waxman, Olivia B. "'We Were in a War Zone': The History of the 1973 Standoff at Wounded Knee." Time, 2023, https://time.com/6276127/wounded-knee-occupation-history/.

As many as 300 FBI agents and US Marshals were stationed around Wounded Knee. The situation resulted in three deaths, over a dozen wounded, and 1,200 arrests.[106] The case received vast media attention and gained the support of many Americans.

The Nebraska Air National Guard and the active-duty US Air Force conducted aerial reconnaissance photography of the site. The South Dakota National Guard maintained the military vehicles during the siege. Between the Army National Guard and the Regular Army, the FBI received 15 armored personnel carriers, 100,000 rounds of M-16 ammunition, 11,000 parachute flares, 20 sniper rifles with scopes, gas masks, bulletproof vests, and other sustainment items.[107]

The issues of military involvement were controversial but settled in court. The court found that the assistance did not violate the Posse Comitatus Act if the military involvement was passive or indirect.[108] The National Guard and Regular Army support during the 1973 Wounded Knee stand-off closely resembled the Waco stand-off 20 years later.[109]

1980 to Present

War on Drugs

President H.W. Bush declared a War on Drugs in 1989 and ordered the Pentagon to use its resources.[110]

The National Guard became the primary link in providing military support to law enforcement agencies and created policies to ensure no violation of Posse Comitatus. The Guard supported law enforcement with reconnaissance and surveillance as well as search and seizure missions on the border but would not directly arrest or confiscate

---

106 Ibid.
107 "Army Tested Secret Civil Disturbance Plan at Wounded Knee, Memos Show." *New York Times Archives,* 1975, https://www.nytimes.com/1975/12/02/archives/army-tested-secret-civil-disturbance-plan-at-wounded-knee-memos.html.
108 "Military Involvement in the Government Operations at Waco." *Cult Education Institute.* House of Representatives Report, 104th Congress, 2nd Session, 1996, https://culteducation.com/group/1220-waco-davidians/24432-military-involvement-in-the-government-operations-at-waco.html.
109 Ibid.
110 Doubler, p. 295

property.[111] The funding for the Guard's Counterdrug Program depended on the condition that it would not interfere with regular combat training.

The military could provide nonrefundable support if there was a drug nexus or if the requesting federal agency believed drugs were involved in the situation.

The Guard Counterdrug Program remains active as of this writing in 2023.

The War on Drugs has been criticized for the militarization of law enforcement.

Ruby Ridge

On August 21, 1992, a stand-off occurred in Ruby Ridge, a mountainous and rural area in North Idaho, between US Marshals and the family of Randy Weaver. An agent and his team were conducting surveillance on the ground near the Weavers' mountain home. Weaver, a separatist, was wanted for illegally selling two sawed-off shotguns and missing court. The situation unraveled after a camouflaged federal agent shot the Weavers' dog. Surprised by the death of their dog, Weaver's son and family friend returned fire. When the fire exchange ended, Sammy Weaver, a 14-year-old boy, and Deputy US Marshal William Francis Degan died. The Weaver family refused to surrender.

Governor Cecil Andrus declared a state of emergency, saying, "The nature of the disaster is the occurrence and the imminent threat of injury and loss of life and property arising out of the stand-off situation in Boundary County."[112]

The Governor's declaration that day allowed law enforcement agencies on the scene to use the local Idaho National Guard's Armory, Armored Personnel Carriers (APCs), and other equipment.[113] The APCs delivered personnel and equipment close to the Weaver home.

---

111 Doubler, p. 295
112 Linder, Douglas O. "Department of Justice Report on Internal Review Regarding the Ruby Ridge Hostage Situations and Shootings by Law Enforcement Personel." *Famous Trials,* DOJ – IV, Specific Issues Investigated (Part H), 1992, https://famous-trials.com/rubyridge/1131-lawenforcement.
113 Ibid.

The stand-off lasted for 11 days. During that time, a crowd of over 100 neighbors, concerned citizens, protestors, and skinheads wearing swastikas began to gather. The mood of the crowd became more critical of the federal government.[114]

Many of the FBI and other federal law enforcement actions, including the Rules of Force, were controversial, and some were found unconstitutional. The televised situation fueled anti-government sentiment in some groups of Americans.

However, using the National Guard during the stand-off at Ruby Ridge didn't result in scrutiny as it did just one year later in Texas.

Waco

The 51-day stand-off at Waco, Texas, was a highly controversial use of military support and tactics. The lasting memory of the situation is the military tanks and personnel supporting the siege.[115]

A religious group led by David Koresh, the Branch Davidians, lived in a compound just outside of Waco, Texas. The Bureau of Alcohol, Tabacco, and Firearms (ATF) believed the community was stockpiling illegal weapons. The raid on the compound went tragically wrong with a shootout that resulted in the deaths of four ATF agents. The situation escalated over 51 days and ended with a tactical compound siege. Untimely, the CS gas (2-chlorobenzylidene malonitrile) pumped into the building ignited a devastating fire, causing the deaths of 80 men, women, and children.

The Texas National Guard Counterdrug Program was part of the initial raid, stand-off, and siege at the Branch Davidian compound in April 1993. After the failed attack in February 1993, the Texas National Guard's limited support dramatically increased to armored personnel carriers, tanks, and combat engineer vehicles to provide safety to law enforcement personnel.[116]

---

114 Olson, Ben. "Stand-Off at Ruby Ridge: 25 Years Later (Part II)." *Sandpoint Reader,* 2017, https://sandpointreader.com/stand-off-ruby-ridge-25-years-later-part-ii/.

115 US Government. "The Tragedy at Waco: New Evidence Examined." *House Report 106-1037,* 106th Congress, 2nd Session, 2000, https://www.govinfo.gov/content/pkg/CRPT-106hrpt1037/html/CRPT-106hrpt1037.htm.

116 Ibid.

The ATF requested the support of the Texas National Guard Counterdrug Program. In their formal request, the ATF indicated the potential for hazardous drug-related material and firearms in the compound. The ATF believed the Davidians were producing methamphetamines. The drug connection was critical for using National Guard assistance under the law.[117]

Texas National Guard provided overflights and compound reconnaissance, flights in support of siege, and warrant services. Personnel included pilots, liaisons, and mechanics for equipment.[118] The Guard supplied cargo trucks, combat engineer vehicles, supplies, helmets, protective masks, and rations. The Texas National Guard requested the support of the Alabama National Guard Counterdrug Program, which provided additional overflights and reconnaissance photography of the compound.

The Texas National Guard loaned Combat Engineering Vehicles (CEV) equipped with mounted CS gas spring devices, which injected gas directly into the compound. The CEVs were used to penetrate the structure.[119] FBI agents operated the military vehicles.

About 100 Texas National Guardsmen and 200 active-duty forces intermittently provided on- and off-site support to the FBI during the stand-off. Under the National Defense Authorization Act of 1991, active-duty forces were authorized to provide counterdrug military assistance to the ATF and FBI. However, it is essential to note that after several investigations, no violations of the Posse Comitatus law were violated by the active duty on the ground.

Some controversy concerns allegations that federal agents fired shots from inside military helicopters. If that is true, the situation was a military assault on civilians. However, this has never been proven.

---

117 Department of Defense. "Military Assistance Provided at Branch Davidian Incident." Report to the Secretary of Defense, the Attorney General, and the Secretary of the Treasury, United States General Accounting Office, 1999. https://www.gao.gov/assets/nsiad/osi-99-133.pdf.

118 Ibid.

119 US Government. "The Tragedy at Waco: New Evidence Examined." *House Report 106-1037*, 106th Congress, 2nd Session, 2000, https://www.govinfo.gov/content/pkg/CRPT-106hrpt1037/html/CRPT-106hrpt1037.htm.

The Alabama and Texas Memorandum of Agreement (MOA) has also been challenged on legality because the MOA is a contract, and the Constitution says only Congress can ratify agreements.

After the incident, the DOD failed to collect details of the mission. The total involvement of the military is not documented.[120]

The Texas and Alabama Guardsmen were on Title 32 status, which meant they were not subject to the Posse Comitatus Act but could provide support to federal law enforcement agencies.[121]

The Governor of Texas indicated she did not approve the Alabama National Guard to enter her state. She wasn't aware of the extent of the Texas National Guard's involvement until after the failed raid. If this were the case, the Alabama National Guard would have no authority to conduct military operations in Texas.

This vital question remains unanswered: Who controlled the National Guard?

Rodney King Riots

In April 1992, south-central Los Angeles erupted in racial tensions after a verdict found an LA policeman innocent in a roadside beating of Rodney King.[122] The Governor called on over 10,000 Guardsmen to restore the peace. However, 53 people died before they could, and the property damages exceeded $800 million. When the Guard deployed, minorities were in the ranks, unlike the Watts Riots in 1965.[123]

Louisville, Kentucky, 2020

The tensions regarding police brutality were already sizzling because of the death of Breonna Taylor on March 13, 2020. Police bullets struck Ms. Taylor six times during a drug raid. At least seven police, wearing civilian clothing, entered her apartment while Ms. Taylor and her boyfriend were sleeping. Breonna's boyfriend believed the police were intruders and fired at them. The police returned fire with

---

120 Ibid.
121 Ibid.
122 Doubler, p. 308
123 Ibid.

approximately 32 rounds in the apartment. The death of Breonna Taylor gained national attention after George Floyd's death.

On May 30, 2020, the governor of Kentucky, Andy Beshear, and several other governors activated their National Guards to help provide safety and protection to the local communities.[124] In Louisville, the mayor wanted a "dusk to dawn" curfew to curtail broken windows, graffiti, fires, and looting.

The mayor said outside groups promoted violence to harm everyone on the streets: "There is an effort going on around the nation to create this kind of disturbance."[125] Brigadier General Hal Lambert, the Adjutant General of the Kentucky National Guard, said, "We will ensure the Kentucky citizens have the right to demonstrate peacefully and safely."

On June 1, 2020, downtown protests dispersed after midnight. Two Louisville Metro Police and two Guardsmen went to the West End, where a large crowd gathered in a parking lot. The law enforcement team planned to enforce the community curfew. The police officers fired pepper balls at Yaya's BBQ restaurant, where the crowd gathered.[126]

The evidence indicates that the owner, Mr. David McAtee, fired two shots from a handgun. The police and the National Guard returned fire. It was determined that one of the National Guard officers shot the only bullet, which struck and killed Mr. McAtee.[127] In total, 19 rounds were fired by the two Guard members and the two Louisville

---

124 Martin, Stephen. "Day Two: Kentucky Guard Activated to Help Protect Kentuckians safety and maintain peace." Ky. Guard News, Kentucky National Guard Public Affairs Office, 31 May 2020, https://ky.ng.mil/News/Article/2722131/day-two-ky-national-guard-activated-to-help-protect-kentuckians-safety-and-main/.

125 Otts, Chris. "Fischer requests National Guard to Louisville, imposes curfew in response to protests." WDRB, 30 May 2020, https://www.wdrb.com/in-depth/fischer-requests-national-guard-to-louisville-imposes-curfew-in-response-to-protests/article_8dac6102-a279-11ea-9ee1-6f80cd88dee7.html.

126 Bennett, Jared. "National Guard Investigation After David McAtee Shooting Still Not Done." Louisville Public Media, 5 May 2021, https://www.lpm.org/investigate/2021-05-05/national-guard-investigation-after-david-mcatee-shooting-still-not-done.

127 Bennett, Jared. "Ky. National Guard Releases Heavily Redacted Review of Louisville Deployment." Louisville Public Media, 18 May 2021, https://www.lpm.org/investigate/2021-05-18/ky-national-guard-releases-heavily-redacted-review-of-louisville-deployment. w

officers.[128] The soldiers used their M-4 rifles while on this domestic support mission.

The McAtee family filed a wrongful death lawsuit over the excessive force that resulted in his death. The case claimed, "The National Guard did not receive proper command, instruction, equipment or training… before being assigned to work in the streets of the city."[129]

After the death, the National Guard released a heavily redacted review of the situation to the media. An independent Indiana Brigadier General study found that the Guard members were prepared and well-trained. However, many questions still needed to be answered. What kind of training did the National Guard have for crowd control? What were the "use of force" instructions for this mission? Were the instructions consistent with state and local law?[130]

Washington, DC, 2020

In June, protestors graffitied a statue of Andrew Jackson in Lafayette Square outside of the White House. About 500 Guardsmen were sent to the DC armory and put on standby to protect the monuments. To use active-duty military would require invoking the 1807 Insurrection Act. Defense Secretary Mark Esper said the National Guard is best suited for domestic support to civil authorities.[131]

The DC Guard received significant criticism for using a low-flying MedEvac helicopter during the protests. After the 7:00 p.m. curfew, protestors of George Floyd's death were still on the streets. A helicopter hovered directly over them and created strong winds, a tactic to show force in a combat zone. A year after the incident, a DOD report found that "no specific training, policies, or procedures were in place for using

128

129 Lovan, Dylan. "Kentucky prosecutor won't seek charges in Guard shooting of Cook." Army Times, 25 May 2021. https://www.armytimes.com/news/your-military/2021/05/25/kentucky-prosecutor-wont-seek-charges-in-guard-shooting-of-cook/.

130 Bennett, Jared. "Ky. National Guard Releases Heavily Redacted Review of Louisville Deployment." Louisville Public Media, 18 May 2021, https://www.lpm.org/investigate/2021-05-18/ky-national-guard-releases-heavily-redacted-review-of-louisville-deployment.

131 Welna, David. "Pentagon Chief Rejects Trump's Threat To Use Military To Quell Unrest." NPR, 3 June 2020, https://www.npr.org/2020/06/03/868929288/pentagon-chief-rejects-trumps-threat-to-use-military-to-quell-unrest0

helicopters to support requests for assistance from civilian authorities in civil disturbances."[132]

The deployment of thousands of Guardsmen nationwide supported local law enforcement in keeping the peace during the large-scale protests.

General Joseph Lengyel called it the "toughest mission in our domestic portfolio."[133]

This was the most significant domestic response in the National Guard's history because of combined COVID-19 and civil unrest problems—more than 90,000 Guards were on duty.

Summary

The National Guard was called upon numerous times during the tumultuous era of the 1960s and 70s when citizens protested their civil rights and the government's involvement in foreign conflicts.

The 1980s significantly increased law enforcement agencies' use of National Guard support. In 1981, Congress passed new legislation allowing the Active and Reserve forces to assist law enforcement with training and equipment, the use of military equipment and facilities, and the use of military personnel. However, direct participation in law enforcement was prohibited.[134] The Guardsmen working in this capacity then and now are under a Title 32 status.

The issue of the National Guard and federal military in the Waco, Texas stand-off illustrates that the military should never be used against the citizens of a nation it supports. For this reason, there is a clear separation between civilian authority and military support for that authority.[135]

---

132 Liebermann, Oren. "Pentagon watchdog finds National Guard's use of helicopters to fly over DC protestors "reasonable," but mired in confusion." *CNN Politics*, 28 May 2021, https://www.cnn.com/2021/05/28/politics/pentagon-national-guard-helicopter-dc-protests.

133 Lengyel, Joseph. "This Is One Of Our Finest Hours." *National Guard Magazine*, 2020, http://www.nationalguardmagazine.com/articles/-this-is-one-of-our-finest-hours-.

134 "Military Involvement in the Government Operations at Waco." *Cult Education Institute*. House of Representatives Report, 104th Congress, 2nd Session, 1996, https://culteducation.com/group/1220-waco-davidians/24432-military-involvement-in-the-government-operations-at-waco.html.

135 Ibid.

In the aftermath of tragedy, questions inevitably arise about what authority was in power, who was giving orders, and what rules of force were in play. Often, in trying to explain how situations spiral out of control, we are left trying to define terms—but the truth is, amid the madness of an angry and frightened crowd, lines may become badly blurred. This is a controversy that may never be perfectly solved. Increased training and social awareness will hopefully help us move forward together.

The 1960s saw violent reactions to social change—but this period is almost sixty years past. Those born decades after might witness the shocking events of Ruby Ridge and Waco or the intensity of Black Lives Matter and political protests during the Trump and Biden administrations and think such events to be unprecedented.

Quite the opposite is true. The United States was born of violent activism, and civil unrest has continued as the United States has evolved. The militia and National Guard have been on the frontlines through it all.

CHAPTER 8

❧

Conclusion

The Minute Man Statue

At the centennial celebration of the Battle of Concord on April 19, 1875, artist Daniel Chester French used Captain Davis as his inspiration to create the Minute Man statue. The bronze statue portrays the elite young volunteer standing tall, his hat brim pinned on the left side. The young man wears a jacket over a button-up shirt with sleeves rolled above the elbow. A horn musket, held tightly, is slung from his left shoulder across his body to his right side. His pants are tucked into his boots with riding protectors. By his side lies a plow and a long coat folded on it. His face, chest, and left leg are pointing toward the left. His gaze is serious.

His confident posture depicts his contemplation of the future fight. The volunteer's right leg is behind his body, with the heel up and slightly turned. The Minute Man is leaving behind his farm, the fields, and the plow and moving bravely toward the unknown fight.

The statue is a fitting symbol of the modern-day National Guard. The plow on the ground represents the soldier's civilian life and connection to the community he is leaving behind. His firm grasp on the rifle and sturdy posture demonstrate his bravery and determination as he moves toward duty. He answers the call to protect his community, a moral and ethical call to serve.

The National Guard in the Past, Present, and Future

The history of the National Guard goes back to early American colonists, who arrived in their new country with the tradition of the militia and Enlightenment ideals.

The citizen-soldier is based on the enlightened idea that individuals are born free and have a right to arm and defend their communities. The original citizen-soldier was driven by the inner calling of duty to their community and the need to protect and preserve their way of life. Citizens picked up arms because of moral responsibility.

The birthdate of the modern National Guard is December 13, 1636, when the Massachusetts government raised the first militia regiment.

The colonists brought their tradition of the militia with John Locke's philosophy of citizens' inalienable rights of life, liberty, and property. As the king's oppression of the colonies increased, so did the dislike and distrust of a standing army. Thus, tensions were planted in our Constitution concerning a standing army versus a militia. Like the hoplites of Athens, the National Guard is a part-time force of men and women in the community.

The original concept of the citizen-soldier service was based on the obligation to the community without pay or benefits: their compensation was safety and preserving a way of life. The first American citizen-soldiers were required to provide their weapons and received no compensation for training.

George Washington knew the political sensitivities around a European-style standing army but believed a small military was needed and affordable. He wrote about the dangers of a large standing army in the time of Peace and the implications to the liberties of a Country. At the time, the distrust and hatred of the Redcoats' standing army dominated defense policy.

The misconception about the National Guard is understandable because of its dual mission. Nevertheless, the uniqueness of the National Guard is intrinsically American. The Founding Fathers tried to thread the needle between the colonial Americans' contempt for the British standing army and the need for an organized national defense in the new country. Over 244 years, the National Guard's dual missions have transformed alongside the United States' emergence as a superpower.

However, the transition and bifurcation of the National Guard to both a domestic and overseas combat force started with the Constitution. The Constitution, while remarkable, established many limitations on the state militias that had to be overcome. It was the founding document that created the militia and almost 250 years of tensions.

The Constitution established a militia and the ability to create a standing Army.

America's wars created the need for a standing Army and the ability to immediately add needed personnel to the force numbers. Yet, the need to grow a federal force fast revealed the weakness inherent in depending on state militias. The laws overseeing the National Guard's ability to fight overseas had to overcome many limitations. At times, the political tensions between the governors and president tested the laws governing the National Guard.

The National Guard's dual mission is the result of the American system of government. From the beginning, the Constitution was designed for compromises and tensions with balances of power. The areas not specified in the Constitution were the responsibility of the state governments. At the time, the militia was the sole responsibility of the states. As the federal government increased the funding of the militias, the requirements to serve overseas in combat also rose. The dual mission of the National Guard evolved and was articulated in legislation.

The National Guard results from over 200 years of compromises and balances of responsibility between the states and the federal government. The National Guard's mission, manning, capabilities, and maturity parallels the story of the American hegemonic era. Today, the misconception about the National Guard is likely due to the use of the National Guard during the US and Vietnam War eras.

During the Vietnam War, President Johnson largely avoided activating the National Guard and Reserve Forces in combat operations. The president operated under the assumption that activating the Reserve components might provoke the Soviets and Chinese to enter the conflict. He purposely wanted to keep the local communities out of the conflict and avoid the secondary impacts of a total mobilization of the National Guard and Reserve forces. Instead, President Johnson opted to fight the war with draftees.

President Johnson's decision undermined and diminished the National Guard's reputation. The Selective Service Act of 1967 had many loopholes to avoid the draft, including joining the National Guard. The Americans alive during the Vietnam War witnessed the National Guard primarily used for civil unrest while the draft augmented the Active Duty conducting combat operations in Southeast Asia. The war, draft, and cultural shifts contributed to the low perception of the National Guard and the US military.

Between 1965 and 1970, the National Guard was enmeshed in civilian unrest at home as they supported the civilian authorities with race and anti-war protests. In 1965, California activated 13,395 National Guard to support the civil authorities during the race riots in Watts, California. A few years later, the violence in Detroit, Michigan, exceeded what the 10,000 National Guardsmen could provide, and President Johnson authorized federal troops to control the city. In 1968, nearly 105,000 Guardsmen were used for riots at different times and places. For the most part, Americans witnessed the National Guard as a domestic force.

The modern-day National Guard is unlike any other military because of the American federal and republican form of government with compromises and tensions over scarce resources.

The National Guard is often called upon to respond to natural disasters or other emergencies within the United States. When activated for federal service, the Guard reports to the president of the United States. When serving in a state capacity, the Guard reports to the governor of that state.

The National Guard has served our country in countless, cost-effective ways, adding depth to our corps, and they've been a part of our country for almost 400 years. The National Guard is the military force that serves right here in the United States. They've coordinated the backbone of our homeland's security. Our Guard helps form a partnership, a handshake between local and federal forces. They are the chain that links our governments together. They've also developed connections with 89 other nations.

General Daniel Hokanson, Chief of the National Guard Bureau, describes the Guard's core missions as "Warfight, Homeland, and Partnerships. These core missions are carried out through four priorities: people, readiness, modernization, and reform."[136]

The primary function of the National Guard is to act as a ready-to-deploy operational reserve. While our primary Army is stationed in critical areas around the globe, our National Guard acts as a backup force that can be placed where needed without disrupting the primary Army. They're the supports under the mighty bridge of our primary forces and are essential to prepare us for the world's complicated, evolving security environment.

Though the Guard has always been an integral part of our country, its presence and purpose in the US were highlighted significantly in 2020. Over 120,000 Guard troops deployed that year to face the combined turmoil of COVID-19 and nationwide political and social justice protests. This degree of Guard mobilization hadn't been seen since World War II.

General Hokanson states, "My goal over the next three years is to build a sustainable operational force by focusing on our core missions— The National Guard Bureau will work in concert with the 54 states, territories, and D.C. to prioritize our efforts." He continued to say, "We must continue to build a National Guard that is stronger and more responsive, a force with greater lethality, global influence, and the combat readiness to deter aggression.

"Today's [National Guard] leaders will have to contend with budget pressures, training shortfalls, time constraints, and modernization gaps. We must develop leaders capable of performing at today's pace of change; redefine how we train forces and approach readiness; and seek

---

136 National Guard Bureau. *Year of the Guard. National Guard,* Posture Statement, 2022, https://www.nationalguard.mil/portals/31/Documents/PostureStatements/2022%20 NGB%20Posture%20Statement-low.pdf?ver=Xwh0Jo8JTB9GlbjTB1H0JQ%3D%3D.

to become more joint and multi-domain-minded. This is critical as we look to normalize the capabilities of an operational National Guard within the DOD's processes."[137]

Always Ready, Always There

The National Guard is a part-time military force that drills typically one weekend a month, along with 15 annual training days. In the 1960s, Americans began referring to the Guardsmen as "weekend warriors" because of their part-time training schedule. The National Guard comprises the Air and Army National Guard units. The Air and Army are part of the Joint National Guard force at the state and National Guard Bureau levels. The National Guard and Reserve forces both serve part-time but have different missions.

Unlike the National Guard, the Reserve forces do not have a state mission. That is, the Reserve forces exist to augment the active-duty forces. The Reserves serve under the direction of the president of the United States. The National Guard is the only citizen-soldier force with the mission to serve their local and global communities.

The citizen-soldier is not a mercenary or part of the professional standing Army isolated from society. The citizen-soldier works and lives in the community and comes from all walks of life and demographics. The citizen-soldier is as diverse as the American people. During any month, the traditional citizen-soldier wears civilian clothes 28 days a month and puts on their military uniform to train one weekend a month.

This book introduced and examined the uniquely American military force of the National Guard. The Guard story coincides with political tensions, the rise of the United States' international dominance, and cultural change domestically. The Guard is interwoven in American history, both good and bad. The Guard includes men and women from all walks of life who come together to serve their community and country. A few members of the National Guard are full-time, providing administrative and operational functions, but most of the National Guard are traditional soldiers with civilian careers. No matter their background or occupation, all members of the National Guard are trained and ready to support their local and global community.

---

137 Ibid.

ABOUT THE AUTHOR

Leslie Wolf is an Idaho National Guard Officer with over thirty years of military officer experience in operations and team management. She holds a Master of Arts in Defense and Strategic Studies from the US Naval War College and a Master of Science in Public Administration from Boise State University. She deployed with the 116th Cavalry Brigade Combat Team in Operation Iraqi Freedom III from 2004 to 2005. She returned with the Brigade to Iraq in Operation New Dawn from 2010 to 2011. She served two and a half years in Cambodia as the Bilateral Affairs Officer through the National Guard State Partnership Program.

Leslie has held various leadership positions in the Idaho Army National Guard. She has two sons, Chaz Gentry and Coleman Gentry. Both Chaz and Coleman have served in the military. In fact, Leslie served in Operation New Dawn with Chaz, her older son. Coleman and her daughter-in-law Laura have two children, Alden and Georgia Gentry. They all hold special places in Leslie's heart.

Leslie enjoys running, golfing, and spending time with her friends and family.